EDUCATING ENGINEERS

Educating Engineers

A History of Engineering Education at Valparaiso University

Edgar J. Luecke

College of Engineering
Valparaiso University
2009

Educating Engineers Copyright © 2009 by Edgar J. Luecke.
Printed in the United States of America. All rights reserved. No Portion of this book may be reproduced in any form or by an electronic or mechanical means including information storage and retrieval systems without permission in written form from the publisher, except by a reviewer, who may quote brief passages in a review to be printed in a magazine, newspaper, or on the Web.

Published by Valparaiso University Press, Valparaiso, IN 46383

First Edition. First printing July 2009.

Cover Design by Becca Spivak-Hendricks
Cover font: Adobe Garamond and Universe
Body font: Palatino
Book Designed and Printed by Home Mountain Publishing Co., Inc.
3602 Enterprise Avenue, Valparaiso, Indiana 46383. (219) 462-6601

Library of Congress Control Number 2009931832

ISBN 978-0-9712294-3-3

Copies of this book may be purchased at Valparaiso University College of Engineering, 1900 Chapel Dr., Valparaiso, IN 46383

To Dorcas

CONTENTS

PREFACE

One	Beginnings: 1859-1873	1
Two	Establishing an Engineering Course: 1873-1900	10
Three	Engineering Achieves a Separate Identity: 1900-1919	25
Four	In Search of New Identities: 1919-1930	44
Five	Promise Meets Reality: 1930-1940	62
Six	A Venture of Faith: 1940-1951	78
Seven	From the Engineering Laboratory to Gellersen Center: 1951-1968	100
Eight	The College Matures: 1968-1985	127
Nine	Responding to Change: 1985-2009	150
Ten	A Look into the Future	172
Appendix A:	Engineering Faculty, 1873 – 2009	177
Appendix B:	Department Heads and Chairs	181
Appendix C:	Engineering National Council Members	182
Appendix D:	Alumni Association Board Members	183
Appendix E:	Enrollment and Degree Data	184
References		188
Index		191

Preface

In September, 1951, I arrived at Valparaiso University as a freshman student in the newly-resurrected four-year engineering program. Like most freshmen, I had no real idea of what it meant to be an engineer and even less of where it would lead me. Whatever I imagined, it surely was not that 58 years later I would still be in Valparaiso after a teaching career at Valpo that spanned 47 years. Knowing of that long tenure, several colleagues have encouraged me, in my retirement, to document the history of the College of Engineering. I resisted for 5 years, but finally my wife, Dorcas, persuaded me that it would be a good project and coaxed me to join her at the university archive, where she was a volunteer, to see what was there. Two and a half years later, this book is the result.

For most of the first 65 years of its history, Valparaiso University was a unique higher education institution. The evidence suggests that for much of that time the engineering course was also unique. For most of the next 85 years it has been unique among Lutheran universities, being the only one to offer standard four-year engineering degrees. Engineering education in the United States is also unique among industrialized nations in that no official national government policy has established its mission and status. To tell the story of Valparaiso engineering education it is necessary to put it in the context of the history of Valparaiso University and of the development of engineering education in the United States.

To conveniently preserve the record, I have documented events that I consider to be major milestones for engineering education at Valparaiso University in detail. For brevity, other significant events are given lesser attention and some are omitted entirely. No doubt there are many other interesting facets of the history that my research failed to uncover. Also, to preserve the record, I have included biographical information about those professors who were chosen to be the academic leaders of the engineering program. I leave it to others to preserve the biographies of all the other professors who have made significant contributions to engineering education at Valparaiso. Writing about one's own contributions is difficult, and I have chosen to do it in the third person.

I leave it to others to judge whether I have done it fairly. The history is divided into nine separate time periods that coincide with significant events or points of transition in the history of the university or the college.

Readers who desire a more complete history of Valparaiso University should read *Flame of Faith, Lamp of Learning – A History of Valparaiso University* by Richard Baepler. I have made liberal use of it in this recounting of events in the university's history. For details about the College of Engineering I have made extensive use of documents and publications in the university archive, not relying only on my own memory. For some time periods there is a wealth of information; for others, much less. I am sure there is still more to be found; more than once I found important information in totally unexpected places. The definitive history of engineering education in the United States remains to be written. I found *The Making of an Engineer – An Illustrated History of Engineering Education in the United States and Canada* by Lawrence P. Grayson to be the most comprehensive source. It was published to commemorate the 100th anniversary of the founding of the American Society for Engineering Education (ASEE). Various reports commissioned by ASEE were also very helpful. A list of references, other than those in the university archive, is contained in an appendix. While I have made every attempt to be accurate, this work is not intended to be a scholarly history. In the interest of readability, I have chosen not to reference sources for specific facts with footnotes or endnotes. As the author of a book I recently read said about the lack of footnotes, "You will just have to trust me."

As in any project of this size, the help of others was necessary and invaluable. First of all I want to thank my wife, Dorcas Borcherding Luecke. Without her encouragement this history would not have been started, much less completed. She was the chief encourager, critic, and proofreader. Her own knowledge of local Valparaiso community history was invaluable. My son Bill provided much early help with proofreading, style, and organization. He has always said that his ideal job would be editor of scientific journals. Professor Judith Miller, Special Collections Librarian of the Christopher Center for Library and

Information Resources, enthusiastically opened the archive to me and found information for me that I would never have found otherwise. Classmates and colleagues since 1951, Merlyn Vocke and Gilbert Lehmann also read portions of the book that coincided with their own personal history at Valparaiso University. Professor Lehmann got me off to a good start by sharing his own collection of College of Engineering archival material. Thanks to Dean Kraig Olejniczak for his encouragement, the use of the college's records and facilities, his careful reading of the manuscript, and for supporting the publishing of this history. Joseph W. Creech, Adjunct Assistant Professor of Humanities and History and Assistant Director of the Lilly Fellows Program, kindly read the manuscript and made helpful suggestions. Finally, I am much indebted to Emeritus Professor Kathleen R. Mullen for her careful editing, attention to style and organization, and proofreading. It is a better book because of her.

Researching and writing this history has been an enjoyable and rewarding experience, even on those days when the research ran into dead-ends or the writing resulted in no net words on paper. For 58 years Valparaiso University has provided me with many interesting opportunities and challenges. This project has been the latest.

Edgar J. Luecke
May, 2009

ONE

BEGINNINGS: 1859-1873

The story of Valparaiso University begins in 1859 with the founding of the Valparaiso Male and Female College by the Methodist Episcopal Conference of Indiana. The Methodists intended to found a college in each congressional district in Indiana and previously had founded Indiana Asbury University in 1837 at Greencastle (later to be called DePauw) and Moore's Hill College in southeastern Indiana in 1854 (relocated to Evansville in 1917 and called Evansville College). Since sentiment in the country, and particularly in Indiana, during the early and mid-19th century was heavily against any kind of publicly funded education at any level, it fell to the churches to found schools to train young people for the professions.

A New College in Northern Indiana

Why choose Valparaiso as a site for a new college? In the 19th century, northwestern Indiana was isolated from the rest of the state by the Grand Kankakee Marsh, which stretched from near South Bend into Illinois. In the northeastern part of the state, the river system connected to the Great Lakes instead of the Ohio River. Hence travel and commerce north and south was neither convenient nor well established. Because of this isolation from the south, northern Indiana was settled by New Yorkers and New Englanders, while Indiana from the Wabash River south was settled by Virginians and Kentuckians. This sociological difference, along with the travel difficulties, contributed to the lack of interest by the more settled southerners to extend their educational influence in this late-developing part of the state.

The northern Indiana counties were organized between 1831 and 1835, and before 1859 opportunities for any kind of advanced education in northern Indiana were limited. LaPorte University was founded in 1841, but by 1851 it was closed due to lack of funds and patronage. Fort Wayne College was founded in 1846 and did exist in 1859 but closed sometime in the 70s or 80s. Colleges in Logansport and Kokomo may have been operating in 1859 but they ceased to exist before 1870. The only surviving college in existence in the northern third of Indiana before 1859 is Notre Dame (1839) in South Bend. Other surviving Indiana colleges in operation in 1859 were Indiana in Bloomington (1823), Hanover (1827), Wabash (1833), DePauw (1837), Franklin (1844), Butler (1858), and Earlham (1859). All except Wabash are in the southern half of the state.

After 25 years of general settlement in northern Indiana, the area was ripe for a new college to serve it. In 1858 the Pittsburgh, Fort Wayne, and Chicago Railroad was completed across northern Indiana from Fort Wayne through Valparaiso to Chicago. This made Valparaiso a place that could be reached more easily by the growing population of the northern tier of counties and from Chicago to the west. Evidently the city leaders of Valparaiso were more persuasive in selling their town as a college site than those from other Northern Indiana communities.

Higher Education in Indiana in the mid-19th Century

In Valparaiso Male and Female College, the city fathers were getting much more than what we would now call a college. From a 21st century perspective, it may be hard to understand mid-19th century education in Indiana and much of the rest of the nation. In addition to college work, many colleges offered elementary and secondary programs. In Indiana this was common at most, if not all, colleges. In fact, the tuition for the elementary and secondary programs was their main source of income. Parents expected to pay to educate their children, so by attracting the college, the Valparaiso community was able to provide education beyond primary schooling.

Not until 1867, eight years after the Valparaiso Male and Female College was founded, did the Indiana Legislature successfully establish a tax-supported system of public education. Even though the first Indiana state constitution called for state-supported schools when it would become financially practical, the idea had never taken hold. The constitution mandated that each county was to be given land which it could sell to support construction of schools, but established no mechanism other than tuition to pay teachers and operating expenses. The responsibility for operating schools fell to churches or private societies and parents at all levels from elementary through college. Movements to provide tax-supported common schools resulted in legislation in 1849 to authorize school taxes. However, the Indiana Supreme Court ruled the effective parts of the act unconstitutional, and the movement to establish tax-supported primary and secondary schools came to a halt; those already established closed. Particularly in southern Indiana tax-supported schools were considered to be pauper schools, and the taxpayers were in no mood to support paupers. Evidently the after-effects of the Civil War shifted attitudes. While the legislation of 1867 was essentially the same as the previous one, no suit contesting its constitutionality was brought until the 1880s. In the intervening years public tax-supported primary and secondary schools gained a solid foothold all over the state. The 1880s suit failed and no more legal attacks threatened public tax-supported education in Indiana.

THE VALPARAISO MALE AND FEMALE COLLEGE

In the spring of 1859, citizens of Valparaiso subscribed over $11,000 and purchased 15 acres that had belonged to Azariah Freeman for the location of a college southeast of the town. This original site is the land south of Freeman Street at the foot of College Avenue At the time no streets connected the town to the site, but these were completed soon after the college opened on Sept. 21, 1859, in a temporary building. While the cost of a permanent building seemed beyond community resources, at the insistence of several community leaders, one was started in April, 1860. This building, at the end of College Street, was located on a bluff that overlooked the newly-constructed railroad track. Expanded by several additions over the years, it housed the administration offices and library until it was destroyed by fire in 1923.

As was common at the time, the college was organized into primary, preparatory, academic, and collegiate departments. The academic department encompassed what we would now call high school. Describing the content and development of the collegiate curriculum of the Valparaiso Male and Female College is a challenge. Many of the records from the early years were lost in the fire in the administration building. The university archive contains only some of the early catalogs. The catalog for the first year, 1859-60, is preserved, but catalogs for the years 1860-64 and 1869-71 are missing.

At the founding of the college, the collegiate program offered a typical classical curriculum strong in Greek, Latin, and mathematics. From the very beginning in 1859, the mathematics curriculum in the Collegiate Department included a course in Mensuration (calculation of areas and volumes) and Surveying taught by J. M. Davis, B. A. This was probably the most practical course that was offered. Surveying is an excellent application of the concepts of trigonometry and geometry, and such a course responded to the practical needs of the rapidly developing region. By 1865 the course was found in the Scientific Curriculum and had been expanded to include spherical trigonometry. Students could earn a B.S. instead of a B.A by taking French and German instead of Greek and Latin. Starting in 1867, the catalogs do not mention surveying, but the math sequence included calculus and a course in mechanics, a natural application of the concepts of calculus. In addition, a course in Natural Philosophy (Physics) was offered.

The catalog of 1867 also listed a course in telegraphy. This course was not part of the regular course offerings, but was offered by G. A. Dodge, the telegraph operator at the local station of the Pittsburgh, Fort Wayne, and Chicago Railroad just west of the campus. The 1868-69 catalog listed 13 students studying telegraphy. Also in this year, the Scientific Course was expanded to three years, with courses in calculus and mechanics in the third year. There was no mention of engineering as a subject.

By the end of the Civil War, the declining enrollment due to the war had put the fledgling college in financial difficulty. In 1867 Reverend Thomas B. Wood assumed the presidency and attacked the enrollment problems with energy. He raised $25,000 in the community to build a women's dormitory addition to the college building, since the student body had become primarily female. But enrollment continued to decline, and President Wood resigned in 1869.

During this period of falling enrollment Indiana established its system of graded, state tax-supported schools. Since people were now being taxed to support schools, they found it unnecessary to financially support denominational schools. Moreover, the 1862 passage by Congress of the Morrill Act, which established a funding process for states to found colleges for "agricultural and mechanical arts," showed increasing interest in practical education rather than the classical program offered by most colleges. The demise of the Valparaiso Male and Female College occurred in 1871 when the city of Valparaiso established its own tax-supported school system. Local students and their tuition for the pre-college classes were lost to the college. In the summer of 1871 classes were discontinued. However, the city maintained the charter and hoped to find a way to put the enterprise on a more solid footing.

The Early History of American Engineering Education

It will be helpful to put the history of engineering education at Valparaiso in the context of the history of engineering education in the United States in the first half of the 19th century. Until the Revolutionary War, the colonies had been forbidden to manufacture any products; their function was to provide raw materials in exchange for manufactured goods from England. This created a significant disincentive to develop home-grown technical expertise. Whatever technical expertise the young country developed was the result of educated Europeans who had immigrated. In 1775, George Washington wrote Congress about the "Want of Engineers to construct the proper Works and direct the Men." In 1776, John Adams called for an academy to teach engineers for the Continental Army. While there were continued calls to establish such an academy, not until 1794 was a school begun at West Point, New York. A fire in 1796 destroyed the buildings, and operation was suspended. Finally, in 1802 the United States Military Academy at West Point was re-established. Sylvanus Thayer became superintendent in 1817; he organized a curriculum based on that of *Ecole Polytechnique* of France which has remained the basis for engineering education in North America. Congress intended that graduates should also be available for engineering projects in the civil sector, so the curriculum included work on bridges, roads, and canals as well as strictly military fortifications.

Also during the Revolutionary War, Congress urged each state to create a Society for the Improvement of Agriculture, Arts, Manufactures, and Commerce as a way to encourage a home grown industry; and again in the early years of the 19th century, noting wasteful agricultural practices and poor infrastructure, it called on each state to establish schools to train men in agricultural and civil engineering. Particularly distressed by the inefficiency of agricultural production, by the 1820s leaders in the states submitted many petitions and memorials to state legislatures to provide instruction to deal with these problems. Unfortunately no states responded to the calls, but several private schools were established. In 1819, Alden Partridge, an early graduate of West Point, established the American Literary, Scientific, and Military Academy in Norwich, Connecticut. In addition to military subjects, it offered instruction in

"Old College Building" in the 1860s

"Civil Engineering, including the construction of Roads, Canals, Locks, and Bridges." This institution became Norwich University in 1834 and continues its tradition of military and engineering education today.

The first school organized primarily to teach technical subjects without military instruction was Rensselaer Institute (now Rensselaer Polytechnic

Institute) in Troy, New York, founded in 1824. When the state of New York declined to fund such a school even with the financial support of Stephan van Rensselaer, he took it upon himself to found the institution himself. Its original purpose was to provide teachers who could go out to the "sons and daughters of farmers and mechanics" and instruct them in better methods. This concept did not last too long: in 1829 the school dropped its original plan of instruction and began a course in civil engineering. By 1835 the Institute was authorized by the state to offer degrees in civil engineering.

Another early program was begun at the University of Virginia. Organized in 1814, it first offered a course in civil engineering in 1833. In 1835 it established a School of Civil Engineering. One of its first professors, William Barton, later became the first president of the Massachusetts Institute of Technology. One of the strong incentives for establishing engineering programs at this time was the boom in railroad construction. A number of other schools and programs were started at this time, but most of them, including the one at Virginia, did not survive the economic downturn that followed the Panic of 1837.

Fifteen engineering programs existed at the end of the Civil War in 1865. Five of these were associated with military colleges (USMA, USNA, Norwich, Virginia Military Institute, and The Citadel), four were in schools specifically founded for practical studies (Rensselaer, Brooklyn, Cooper Union, and the Polytechnic of Pennsylvania), and six were in traditional colleges (Dartmouth, Yale, New York, Union, Brown, and Michigan). Only the University of Michigan was west of the Appalachian Mountains.

The defining characteristic of all of these programs was the influence of the French system of technical education. The curriculum of the military academies, based on the French model which put technical education in the context of a broader general undergraduate education, became the template for American colleges. Those programs started in the existing colleges were organized in the context of the typical classical education, which required a solid general education. Even Rensselaer, which had started with a different model, reorganized its curriculum in 1849 along the lines of the French *Ecole Centrale* and the developing American system. Engineering was clearly an undergraduate subject in which specialization occurred only after a general education in the arts and sciences.

THE MORRILL ACT

In the period leading up to the Civil War, the value of a formal education in civil engineering was generally accepted, but no programs had been proposed for any of the mechanical arts. Heavily influenced by English practice, schooling in the mechanical arts remained entirely in the apprentice system. Engineering meant only surveying and construction of roads, railroads, bridges, and canals. Representatives from the northern states made several attempts to enable each state to establish colleges for the mechanical arts and agriculture, but these attempts were blocked by the southerners. With representatives from the Confederate States absent, Congress passed the Morrill Act in 1862. According to the Act, each state received 30,000 acres of federal land for each member of congress as determined by the 1860 census. Each state could sell this land to finance colleges of agriculture and mechanical arts.

The influence of existing civil engineering curricula, which were offered in the context of a general education, can be seen in the phrase found in the Morrill Act: "to promote the *liberal* [italics added] and practical education of the industrial classes in their several pursuits and professional life." Several of the early land-grant universities were originally called industrial universities, and many were called Agricultural and Mechanical colleges. For states west of the Appalachians, the Morrill Act stimulated the creation of programs in civil engineering in these new colleges. As a result engineering education grew rapidly after the Civil War: according to a Carnegie Foundation report, there were 41 engineering programs by 1871, 70 in 1872 and 85 by 1880. In the upper Midwest, the land grant universities are The Ohio State University, Michigan State University, Purdue University, University of Illinois, University of Wisconsin, University of Minnesota, University of Missouri, and Iowa State University (which had been founded in 1859 as an agricultural college).

The Indiana General Assembly decided to participate in the Morrill Act in 1865 but waited until 1869 to decide to locate the state's land-grant institution near Lafayette. A grant of $150,000 from John Purdue greatly influenced this decision. The charter of the new university was to "teach agriculture and mechanical arts" and classes began in September, 1874. Rose Polytechnic Institute, founded in 1874 as the Terre Haute School of Industrial Science, began offering classes in 1883. According to the 1892 *History of Education in Indiana*, "with the exception of Purdue it is the only high grade technical or industrial school in the state." Evidently Valparaiso and Notre Dame, both of which had civil engineering courses in the 1880s, did not make the cut.

TWO

ESTABLISHING AN ENGINEERING COURSE: 1873 – 1900

In 1873, the vacant school in Valparaiso reopened as the Northern Indiana Normal School, a private enterprise founded and owned by Henry B. Brown. A recent graduate of the National Normal College of Lebanon, Ohio, he was teaching at the Northwest Normal School at Republic, Ohio (neither of these institutions now exists), but desired to start and operate a school based on his ideas for education. Even though the Valparaiso Male and Female College had suspended operations in 1871, its state charter had been maintained by civic leaders in Valparaiso. Learning from a student at Northwest Normal who had attended Valparaiso Male and Female College that a building and a charter were available in Valparaiso, he investigated. After a visit in the summer of 1873, he persuaded the Valparaiso civic leaders who held the charter to allow him to use the building with the agreement that he would purchase the school when it became successful. In September, he and four associates from the National Normal and Northwest Normal opened for classes, offering a course of study similar to that of the Male and Female College and adding a course in pedagogy. He started with 35 students, many of whom came with him from Northwest Normal.

The rapid expansion of tax-supported primary and secondary education, which was the main cause of the demise of the Valparaiso Male and Female College, became the opportunity for its rebirth as the Northern Indiana Normal School (NINS). The term "normal school" for institutions that trained teachers for what were then called common schools was in general use until the mid-20th century. Because these schools generally had only a two-year curriculum, the educational establishment often denigrated them either as unnecessary or, at best, second-rate. At the time of the founding of the Northern Indiana Normal School, the only other teacher training schools in Indiana were the Fort Wayne and Indianapolis City Training Schools and the State Normal School in Terre Haute (now Indiana State University), which was founded in 1870. A market was waiting to be satisfied.

An Engineering Course is Begun

Always alert to needs that he could meet, Brown wasted little time before introducing an embryonic engineering course. The 1874 catalog listed a Scientific Year set of courses that included a mathematics course in Astronomy, Surveying, and Engineering. No information was given as to what topics were included in this course. With the reopening of the college, G. A. Dodge again offered a telegraphy course, which now included training in the duties of a railroad station agent. This course was unrelated to engineering.

By 1876 the considerably expanded catalog reflected the success of the college. An Engineering Department was listed separately. The following is its complete description: "In this department the very best instruments will be used. The student will have actual practice in the field, so that on completing the work, which can be done in a short time, he will be fully prepared to enter the duties of County Surveyor or Civil Engineer. We know of no other place where equal opportunities are offered for gaining a practical knowledge of these subjects in so short a time. The manner in which a subject is presented, not the time, makes perfect. In Surveying and Engineering, there will be classes in which the BEST instruments will be used."

In 1877 Brown renamed his school as Northern Indiana Normal School and Business Institute. The business course was much like the telegraphy course in that it limited its instruction to the practical training necessary to work in a variety of business offices. The following year, he re-chartered the Northern Indiana Normal School and Business Institute with the State of Indiana to offer twelve programs: Preparatory, Teachers, Business, Collegiate, Law, Medical, Engineering, Music, Fine Arts, Phonographic, Telegraphic, and Review. Not all of these programs were available immediately, but clearly he had big plans for his school.

The expanded catalog for 1878 listed a "Board of Instruction" for the programs that were offered. For the Engineering Department, the Board of Instruction consisted of H. B. Brown, Principal; M. E. Bogarte, mathematics, surveying and engineering; W. A. Yohn, natural sciences;

M. E. Baldwin, rhetoric and geography; L. E. Ward, English composition; and E. J. Miller, drawing – mechanical, architectural, and projection. Martin E. Bogarte and Mantie E. Baldwin were two of the four founders who had accompanied Brown from Ohio. W. A. Yohn was one of the first graduates of the NINS. The 1878 catalog retained the 1876 statements about the Engineering Department and added: "STUDIES AND PRACTICE: Trigonometry, Surveying, Plane Measurement, Resurveys, Government Surveys. Practical engineering — Bridges, Tunnels, Embankments, Excavations, Leveling, Curves, etc. Field Practice and Plotting." The course focused on surveying and its application to road and railway construction, a fitting response to the explosive growth of the railroad industry.

During 1878-79, Professor Bogarte took a year's leave to study engineering and mathematics at the Massachusetts Institute of Technology and elocution at Boston University where he earned an M. A. Soon after his return in 1880, the Engineering Department became the Civil Engineering Department with the following description: "Civil Engineering Department: Land Surveying and Triangulation, Leveling, Circular and Parabolic Curves, Location of Towns. Students will also make a detailed survey for a railroad from running of the preliminary lines to the laying of the rails. All the surveys are carefully plotted and represented on finished plans, also the necessary computations of earth work, horizontal and vertical curves, etc. are made in the class room. The subjects of general statistics [misspelled for statics many catalog years into the future], hydraulics, water supply, drainage, bridges and roofs, strength of materials, structures, etc. are thoroughly discussed in the class room. Astronomy is taken from the Scientific Course. Much attention is given to drawing, as this is considered a very important part of the engineer's work." The addition of static mechanics, strength of materials, and hydraulics aligned the NINS course more closely with the typical civil engineering course of 1880.

To promote the engineering course, the catalog included a comparison of costs.

At Other Schools		At NINS	
Tuition – Eastern Schools	$150-200	Tuition – Full Course	$25
Tuition – Western Schools	$125		
Books, drawing materials	$40	Books, etc.	$8
Board and Lodging	$150	Board and Lodging	$70
English Branches	$40	English Course	Free
Total	$355	Total	$103

President Brown was serious about offering a no-frills, efficient, and low-cost alternative to traditional colleges. He and Professor Bogarte considered the program a standard Civil Engineering program that could compete with established colleges.

Engineering Curricula in 1880

Just what constituted a civil engineering course in 1880 is a somewhat difficult question to answer. The Society for the Promotion of Engineering Education (now the American Society for Engineering Education) conducted an extensive study of engineering education during the 1920s, "Report of the Investigation of Engineering Education 1923-1929." Part of the study traced trends in curricula starting in 1870. The authors, noting that catalog descriptions in the 1870s "left specificity in short supply," estimated that all engineering-related courses beyond mathematics and science constituted about one-third of the typical collegiate program. Often the total course was completed in three years. Details of what an NINS civil engineering student would take also left specificity in very short supply. There is much evidence that these students were considered part of what the NINS called the Scientific Year; certainly much of basic knowledge necessary for success in the civil engineering course was taught in the scientific course. President Brown's philosophy of education was to provide whatever each student needed or wanted: "students should be permitted to enter at any time, select their studies and advance as rapidly as they might be able." In other words, courses had no prerequisites, a situation which complicates our understanding of the curriculum. Students could take as much or as little course work in any subject as suited their objectives as long as they could meet the high standards of the course. It is clear from the description of the Scientific Course that those who wanted an engineering education comparable to those at the more traditional colleges could get it by selecting the Scientific Course and the Civil Engineering Course.

An earlier (1919) report, "A Study of Engineering Education" (usually called the Mann Report after its author Charles Mann), was prepared for the Joint Committee on Engineering Education of the National Engineering Societies. Documenting civil engineering curricula for MIT and Illinois Industrial University (University of Illinois), it showed that both programs were based on the curricula at Rensselaer Polytechnic Institute and the *Ecole Polytechnique*. The following table lists the Scientific and Engineering courses at NINS and the comparable courses at MIT and Illinois.

NINS	MIT	ILLINOIS
Algebra and Geometry	Algebra	Algebra and Geometry
Trigonometry and Analytic Geometry	Trigonometry, Solid, and Analytic Geometry	Trigonometry Analytic Geometry
Botany and Geology		Botany
Physiology		
Latin	Foreign Language	Foreign Language
Rhetoric and Essays		English
Debating		
English Literature	English	
Calculus	Calculus and Applied Mechanics	Calculus
Physics	Physics	Physics
Chemistry	Chemistry	Chemistry
Astronomy, Surveying, and Engineering	Astronomy & Surveying	Surveying & Astronomy
US Government		History
Drawing	Mechanical and Free-hand Drawing, Descriptive Geometry	Descriptive Geometry Drawing Shades and Shadows
Static Mechanics	Elementary Mechanics	Analytic Mechanics
Railroad Surveying	Railroad Surveying	Railroad Surveying
Hydraulics	Hydrographic Surveying	
Structures	Earthwork and Masonry	

For none of the colleges is any information available about the amount of class instruction spent on each of these subjects. Neither is there definitive evidence that engineering students did take both the Scientific Course and the Engineering Course at NINS. The 1880 catalog stated that completion of the Scientific Course required 50 weeks of study and the Engineering Course 22 weeks. This ratio of time was consistent with engineering curricula at other colleges that required about one-third of the program for engineering courses.

In 1880, the catalog for the first time listed the names of students who had studied a particular course in the previous year. In addition to the Preparatory Course, the other six listed courses of the NINS were Classical, Scientific, Teacher, Engineering, Musical, and Fine Arts. Student names were listed for each of these courses except Engineering. With little reason to assume that he would not list every student that attended his school (even students in the allied schools of telegraphy and law were listed), Brown's editorial choice here supports the idea that engineering students were considered part of the Scientific Course. The early catalogs also do not indicate how the Engineering Department fit into the organization of the NINS, but the typeface and organizational layout of later catalogs more clearly puts it in the context of the Scientific Course organization. In fact, one of the two pictures in the 1898 yearbook of the Scientific Course

Martin Eugene Bogarte

The history of The College of Engineering at Valparaiso begins with Martin Bogarte. Professor Bogarte was born on a farm near Republic in north central Ohio on May 3, 1853 or 1855. Most sources list the 1855 date but the Porter County, Indiana death records list 1853. Sources are contradictory about where he was educated, but according to the May, 1911, *Valparaiso Engineering Annual* published under his supervision, he was a graduate of Northwestern Normal and Training School in Republic. The history of this school is scant, but evidently it was moved to Fostoria, Ohio, in 1874 and shortly thereafter failed financially.

One of his teachers there was Henry Baker Brown, who had graduated from National Normal School at Lebanon, Ohio, in 1871. The founder and principal of Northwestern Normal was J. Fraise Richards, who had been a teacher at National Normal. He brought Brown and Samantha Baldwin along with him

Continued next page

showed Prof. Bogarte and his surveying class. Not until 1909 did the catalog list engineering students separately. For our purposes this omission is unfortunate, since we have no way of knowing how many students were typically enrolled in the engineering program.

The Northern Indiana Normal School Grows and Expands

Throughout the 1880s the Northern Indiana Normal School and Business Institute continued to grow. In 1880 the first reference to a Law Department, started in 1879, appeared in the catalog. It was staffed by H. A. Gillette, Circuit Judge of the 31st district; Mark DeMotte, A.M., LL.B.; and W. A. Yohn, M.D., Lecturer of Medical Jurisprudence. It was a separate business operated by Professor DeMotte in much the same fashion as George Dodge operated his telegraphy school. Under the umbrella of the NINS, these departments paid a percentage of their gross tuition receipts to Brown. W. A. Yohn, the natural science instructor in the Engineering Course, had by this time earned an M.D. degree. In this same year the catalog indicated that in the years of operation, the college enrollment had increased from 61 to 1723 students who attended for some time during the year.

Already in 1875 two residence halls, East and Flint, had been constructed. Flint is the only building built before 1935 to survive in 2009. Now known

---

to Republic. In 1873 when Brown took over the closed Valparaiso Male and Female College, he was joined by both Martin Bogarte and Samantha Baldwin and students from Northwestern. Their defection to Valparaiso probably caused the failure of Northwestern Normal.

Martin Bogarte's two great academic passions were mathematics and elocution. He was recognized by all of his students as an extraordinary teacher; it was reported that as many as 900 students a year attended his lectures in elocution. Also, for many years he taught a Sunday school class at the local Christian Church that some said was the second largest in the country. The only publication that survives is his *Manual of Elocution*, but the course catalogs refer also to his geometry text. In mathematics, the only surviving record of his work is a short article in the *Valparaiso Engineering Annual*. It presents a very readable geometric explanation of how to generalize to the fourth dimension.

In 1878 he married Lillian Chamberlain from his home town of Republic. She was a music teacher at the NINS. The two of them set off for Boston for the 1878-79 school-year where she studied music at Boston University and he

as Heritage Hall, it is on the National Register of Historic Places and serves as a secondary building for the Law School. In about 1879 a large building at the northwest corner of College and Union, called Commerce Hall, was constructed to replace a residence hall that had burned. It contained classrooms for the Business Institute and the Fine Arts Course on the third floor, residence rooms on the second floor, and kitchen and dining areas on the ground floor. In 1928 it became the home of the College of Engineering.

The decade of the 1890s, too, was a period of continued growth. Enrollment reached 3000 students in 1897, a size unheard of among colleges and universities at the time. The original college building had been enlarged several times, and in 1892 the Chapel Hall was completed. Its seating capacity of 2500 was chosen to fit the enrollment at the time. In later years it was known as the Auditorium and was destroyed by fire in 1956. In the same year, B. F. Perrine, the other founder of the Normal School along with Brown, Baldwin, and Bogarte, constructed a bookstore building at the southeast corner of College and College Place across from the new Chapel Hall. In 1894 he sold it to Martin Bogarte who then operated it as the M. E. Bogarte Bookstore. He leased part of the space to a print shop which included textbook publishing as part of its business. There is inferential evidence from photographs that the engineering and surveying courses were taught in this building.

---

divided his time between Boston University for elocution and the Massachusetts Institute of Technology for mathematics and engineering. Their son M. Bruce was also a member of the mathematics faculty after graduation from Valparaiso University.

Professor Bogarte was man of enormous energy. In addition to his responsibilities as head of mathematics and engineering instruction, he soon became the owner and operator of the college's book store and print shop, the M. E. Bogarte Book Store. Some time in the 1890s he turned over elocution studies to other faculty and concentrated on mathematics and engineering. One source in the Valparaiso University archive states that he was dean of the civil engineering department in 1900, but the title does not appear in any Valparaiso University catalog. In 1900 he took an extended tour of Europe, Egypt, and the Holy Land and gave a number of lectures about his experience upon his return. During this period he was also a member of the Valparaiso City Council and a stockholder in the Valparaiso National Bank. He is also listed as the president of the Gary Trust and Savings Bank during the early

Continued next page

Surveying Class of 1899. The woman next to Prof. Bogarte is Mrs. J. B. Dolson, who was most likely the drawing instructor.

Instructional departments were also being added. The 1895 catalog lists Pharmacy, started by Professor Evans, plus Biology, Geology and Mineralogy, and English. The Telegraphic Department reappeared with G.

> years of the city's existence. He apparently also had a financial interest in Valparaiso University. When Valparaiso College was re-chartered as Valparaiso University in 1905, a certificate issued by the Indiana Secretary of State lists him along with Mr. and Mrs. Brown and Mr. and Mrs. Kinsey as owners of the business. In 1904, he turned over the day-to-day responsibility for the engineering courses to A. A. Williams, another mathematics professor, but stayed actively involved in the program as its dean while it was converted to a full four-year program. Of course, true to the Valparaiso mission, this program was done in three years of 48 weeks of classes.
>
> After his wife Lillian died, in 1905 he married widow Lida Axe Homfeld. Lida was the daughter of a cousin of Neva Axe Brown, the wife of President Brown. On November 17, 1911, Professor Bogarte died suddenly and unexpectedly of a heart attack. Earlier in the day he had given the chapel address. His death was a great shock to the university; he was the first of the founding five to die. The tribute in the *Valparaiso Daily Vidette* said, "He lived nobly and died peacefully." At his funeral, the paper reported that "the engineers, the bone of his bone and the blood of his blood, were sorely stricken. By virtue of his connection with them, they were given seats at the funeral service ... just behind the faculty."

A. Dodge as Director and his son, G. H. Dodge, as Instructor in 1891. But by 1894, a disagreement between the Dodges and President Brown led to the founding of the independent Dodge Institute of Telegraphy, which in later years became the Valparaiso Technical Institute.

Despite the growth and development of civil engineering programs at other schools in this era, the course descriptions for the Engineering Department remained unchanged. In 1890, the faculty for Civil Engineering numbered six: Martin E. Bogarte, higher mathematics, surveying, engineering; Horace M. Evans, natural science; Miss Mantie E. Baldwin, rhetoric; Mrs. Sarah Kinsey, geography; Miss Lizzie McAlilly, English composition; and Miss Jennie Manchester, drawing. Although the course description did not change, evidently the content did, because the 1890 catalog announced that the course now required a full year instead of 22 weeks. This increase was consistent with national trends in which time spent on engineering courses was increased at the expense of foreign language courses.

Reflecting this growth in size and breadth of the NINS, the format of the 1897 catalog was completely revised. The Scientific Course now required three years of five 10-week terms each year. These 150 weeks of instruction equaled or exceeded the time required for the typical four-year college degree program. The organization of the 1898 catalog clearly places both Surveying and Civil Engineering in the Scientific Course. A 20-week course in Plane Surveying is described in detail: "Besides daily instruction in the classroom, a student has about five months practice in the field and works with proper instruments, for himself, the problems discussed in class. He learns to lay out and divide up land, to run roads and ditches, take levels for profiles and contours, triangulation, to lay out railway curves, vertical and horizontal, to compute earthwork, etc. etc. Very thorough instruction, extending throughout the entire year, is given in mechanical drawing. Text: Carhart's Surveying, Johnson's Surveying, Hodgman's Manual, Gillespie's Surveying – Revised Edition, Henck's Field Book."

Of related interest is the description of the physics course, no longer called Natural Philosophy, which indicates that it was organized in the standard form of Mechanics, Heat, Sound, Electricity and Magnetism, and Light.

The description includes a statement that the course is useful for teachers and those who want to prepare for courses in engineering.

Late 19th Century Engineering Education in America

While the program at the NINS remained limited to civil engineering, engineering education at other colleges was rapidly expanding its offerings in mechanical, and then electrical and chemical engineering and seeking for itself a significant role in preparing young men for engineering careers. At issue was the tension between the accepted role for some formal education for civil and mining engineering and the apprentice system in the mechanical arts. Even in the late 19th century, formal engineering education was neither required nor expected for membership in the professional engineering societies. While attitudes were starting to change, both law and medicine still considered it an acceptable practice for one to apprentice himself to a practitioner. The emerging engineering profession followed the same model. Indeed, it was quite common for engineering professional societies to give no credit for college work toward the hours of experience required for membership. Particularly in the new field of mechanical engineering, contemporary engineering practitioners held to the apprenticeship model and criticized engineering education as not practical enough and taught by instructors with little or no practical experience.

In the years immediately after the conclusion of the Civil War in 1865, the eastern states rapidly industrialized. In 1876, the only two existing professional engineering societies, the civil engineers and the mining engineers, met jointly during the Centennial Exhibition in Philadelphia to consider the future of engineering education for an industrialized society. Men who called themselves mechanical engineers had come through the apprentice system as craftsmen. Those who wished to professionalize mechanical engineering by promoting academic training naturally felt that it was necessary for students to also have significant exposure to the skills of the craftsman. It was clear that the emerging mechanical and electrical technologies could not be accommodated in the existing scheme of engineering education at established colleges. Two competing views of what should constitute an engineering education emerged at the meeting. One view rejected a role for practical training and held that the schools should teach the theory and let the job teach the practice. The other took the view that practical skills such as productive shopwork should be a significant part of the college education.

Two schools that typified this practical training approach were Worchester Free Institute and the Terre Haute School of Industrial Science. The Worcester Free Institute, now Worcester Polytechnic, was founded in 1868 and epitomized the shop approach to engineering education. Its founding objective was "to be based upon the practical mathematics and the application of physical science to the various arts and manufactures, together with other branches of active business." It was organized around a shop staffed by journeymen with whom the students worked to produce items to be sold on the open market. (The University of Illinois, when it was still the Illinois Industrial College, also used a system of manufacturing products that had been designed in the drafting room.) In Indiana, the Terre Haute School of Industrial Science, now Rose Hulman Institute of Technology, opened for classes in 1883. Its first President, C. O. Thompson, had organized the shops at Worcester. In his inaugural address, he described rather well the objective of this kind of education. "The more the students understand the nature and difficulties of the practice, and the more they use theoretical principles as like as possible to those of real practice, the greater are the chances of becoming competent and successful engineers. For best results, the student's work must be subjected to the inexorable tests of business. Without the construction of articles whose workmanship is subjected to the objective test of salability in the open market, shopwork is liable to exalt the purely abstract aspect of mechanical knowledge."

This attitude about shop experience was reinforced by what many engineering educators had seen at the Centennial Exhibition. In addition to the impressive mechanical technology on display, they took note of the Russian exhibit that featured its method of manual training for engineers. Impressed by this approach, the Worcester example, and the growing importance of mechanical engineering, many educators began to incorporate shopwork into their curricula. This represented a significant departure from the engineering programs that had developed out of classical and scientific courses at existing colleges. Except for surveying, the usual method of instruction had been lecture, demonstration, and recitation. Laboratories and shops were to be found only in rare instances.

As an alternative to shopwork, Stevens Institute of Technology, which opened for classes in 1870 to "teach mechanical engineering firmly grounded on sound scientific principles," is recognized as having developed the first laboratory organized for instruction and research. The laboratory was developed by Professor Robert Thurston, a prolific author of engineering textbooks, who is also thought to be the first engineering teacher to conduct sponsored research. Only a few years earlier in 1869 at MIT, the first laboratory for physics instruction was instituted. It was not until the early 20th century that a synthesis of these two approaches, practical shopwork and instruction laboratories, was achieved. The amount of shopwork required of all students reached its maximum in the 1890s and then declined to an amount that remained stable for the next 50 years.

By the early 1890s, mechanical engineering had become a firmly established course in most colleges that offered engineering programs, and electrical engineering was rapidly being introduced. The first degrees in mechanical engineering had been awarded at Polytechnic College of Pennsylvania at Philadelphia in 1854, a college that closed in the mid-1880s. Yale, MIT, and Worcester followed in the 1860s. In the 1880s electrical engineering courses were being developed as an outgrowth of physics departments. MIT offered the first electrical engineering program in 1882, and several other colleges soon followed. The rapid growth of these two specialties can be seen in the organization of two additional professional societies, the American Society of Mechanical Engineers in 1880 and the American Institute of Electrical Engineers in 1884.

The Society for the Promotion of Engineering Education is Founded

Seventeen years after the Centennial Exposition in Philadelphia had showcased the beginnings of the transformation of America from an agrarian society to an industrial society, Chicago held the World's Columbian Exposition in 1893. While a year late in commemorating Columbus's voyage to the New World, it was an unparalleled success, drawing some 12 million visitors. It was said that the scale of the Manufacturer's Building was so vast that no one individual had ever seen all of the exhibits. The site was popularly called the White City for the color of its buildings and the extravagant use of electric lighting. American technology and engineering were on full display.

In this context of rapid technological developments, establishment of new engineering programs, and basic disagreements on what the content of a good engineering education should be, a significant event in the history of engineering education occurred. The organizers of the World's Columbian Exposition invited every organization and profession that they could think of to assemble in "congresses" during the run of the fair. One such congress was the International Congress of Engineering. Ira Osborn, a professor at the University of Illinois, persuaded the organizers to include sessions specifically on engineering education in addition to discipline-specific sessions. Out of this session, the Society for the Promotion of Engineering Education (SPEE) was born. Engineering became the first profession to have a society dedicated to concerns of education for the profession. In later years the name was changed to the American Society for Engineering Education (ASEE).

The attendees at this meeting were for the most part young professors from leading colleges. In addition to establishing a publication in which they could share ways to improve instruction, they recognized a need to bring some order and organization into the teaching of engineering. An 1892 survey by the United States Bureau of Education had found 101 engineering schools but raised concerns that many were of questionable quality. An 1896 survey of entrance requirements found that only 64 of 110 engineering colleges required mathematics beyond algebra through quadratics and plane geometry. As it grew in membership, prominence, and influence in engineering education, the Society at its 1907 annual meeting in Cleveland invited the major professional engineering societies to join it in an examination of all branches of engineering education to, among other things, "formulate a report or reports on the proper scope of engineering education." It would be eleven years before the report was completed. Its conclusions will be outlined in the next chapter.

The M.E. Bogarte Book Store sometime before 1906.

Three

Engineering Achieves a Separate Identity: 1900-1919

Brown and Bogarte must have attended the World's Columbian Exposition in Chicago at least once and probably several times as it was no more than an hour's train ride from Valparaiso. Yet with all the new technology on display, these leaders made no moves to include mechanical, electrical, or chemical engineering in the Valparaiso course offerings. Engineering at Valparaiso remained a civil engineering curriculum centered on surveying, drawing, and railroad construction. So innovative and entrepreneurial in many other areas, they completely missed or dismissed this rapid development in engineering education. Not until the mid-teens did they move to correct this serious omission.

The Northern Indiana Normal School and Business Institute Becomes Valparaiso University

However, in other areas at the turn of the century, the Northern Indiana Normal School and Business Institute was on a roll. New programs were being added, and enrollment continued to increase. To better reflect the school's new mission, Brown re-branded it, first as Valparaiso College in 1900, and then as Valparaiso University in 1905.

With growing programs in science, pharmacy, and civil engineering and Brown's continued desire to have a medical program, a new building, the entry lintel prominently labeled SCIENCE, was completed in 1900, directly west of the main college building. In 1902, Valparaiso College acquired a medical school in downtown Chicago from Northwestern University and renamed it the American College of Medicine and Surgery. Students were to complete the initial portion of the medical program on the Valparaiso campus and then move to Chicago to finish their studies. Some faculty and students commuted to Chicago using special rates on the Pennsylvania Railroad.

A year later Valparaiso College purchased the American College of Dental Surgery in Chicago. To house the work of the medical and pharmacy programs, the Medical Building was completed directly west of the Science building in 1906. In this same year, the new building for the extensive music program was erected directly east of the Chapel Hall/Auditorium with a prominent MUSIC on its entry lintel. A 1907 campus map shows 25 buildings in the campus neighborhood. Nine were instructional buildings and the rest were residence halls of varying quality.

The scope of the academic offerings and the organization of Valparaiso University can be seen from the listing of enrolled students and graduates in the 1906 catalog. Students were listed in seventeen departments, not all of which awarded diplomas. The departments (with the number of graduates in parentheses) were: Preparatory (0), Teachers (0), Collegiate-Classics (18), Collegiate-Scientific (93), Psychology and Pedagogy (10), Commercial (208), Special Penmanship (0), Law (67), Pharmacy (68), Medical (80), Dental (90), Musical (18), Elocution and Oratory (7), Phonographic (0), Art (0), Kindergarten (3), and Manual Training (0). Engineering courses and students were still part of the Collegiate-Scientific program.

The Manual Training Course had been added in 1903 at the urging of the State of Indiana to meet the growing need for manual training teachers in high schools. The necessary woodworking and metalworking shop equipment was installed on the ground floor of the south wing of the Commerce Building. The catalog stated that the courses were suitable not only for future teachers, but also for those studying engineering. In 1906, a separate Manual Training Department was established with 120 students.

CIVIL ENGINEERING MOVES TO THE MAINSTREAM

When he re-chartered the NINS in 1878, President Brown clearly intended to have an engineering program, but, for whatever reason, it evidently was not his highest priority. Perhaps no champion emerged who was willing or able to expend the considerable energy necessary to organize a new course of studies. Professor Bogarte clearly had engineering dear to his heart, but his involvement in so many ventures on and off the campus probably precluded his keeping the civil engineering course up-to-date or adding additional engineering programs. All evidence is that his civil engineering course, while being increased in duration, had not responded to most of the evolutionary changes that had occurred between 1880 and 1900. Not until 1904 were there signs of change.

The addition of courses and shops for manual training created an opportunity to expand the engineering course and bring it closer to mainstream engineering curricula. By the 1890s, most engineering schools had added degree programs in mechanical and electrical engineering, programs greatly influenced by the practical shop orientation of programs such as those at Worcester Polytechnic and Rose Polytechnic. Although there was no clear consensus as to the amount, leading engineering educators believed some shop work was central to a modern engineering program, even for civil engineers.

Some of the history of the development of the CE course at Valparaiso may be best described by recounting a short history included in the Engineering portion of the 1915 *Record*, the University yearbook.

> The Engineering Department in its present stage of development is but 6 years old. Its beginning dates back to 1883, when our late beloved Dean, M. E. Bogarte, who had taught elocution, mathematics and penmanship for nine years at Valparaiso University, installed plane and topographical surveying courses. Each course covered 12 weeks and included about two-thirds of what is now done in the same time. ... For twenty-one years he administered with remarkable skill to the Embryo Engineers this most important branch of their work. In 1904 Prof. Bogarte's duties as Head of the Mathematics Department, the management of the Book Store, his wonderful success in the Christian Sunday School and his regular five hours teaching, including surveying every school day was too heavy a load for even a strong man to carry. Accordingly he transferred

the engineering work to the able shoulders of our most earnest teacher, Prof. A. A. Williams. He had time to improve the course and required for the work seven hours a day through two terms. In this time, not only Plane surveying and Topography were taught, but Railway Location and Construction as well. Along with the above work the regular academic work as mathematics, science, literature and history were required. During the years 1905-1909 inclusive, Mr. Bogarte's classes averaged probably 25 students, while Mr. Williams' averaged about 35. The inception of the present department was the result of plans worked out by Profs. Bogarte, Williams, Cloud, and Black.

Actually, surveying and engineering were first offered in 1874 and engineering as a separate course was instituted in 1880.

Alpheus A. Williams, a NINS graduate, was a mathematics professor who had taken a leave in 1904 to do graduate work in engineering at the University of Illinois. Also a NINS graduate, John H. Cloud was Head of the Physics Department who did graduate work at Johns Hopkins and the University of Chicago. Various references credit him with a Ph. D. but do not list where or when he earned it. Copies of a physics text that he authored are in the university archive. Homer Black was the Head of the Manual Training Department.

ALPHEUS AMERICUS WILLIAMS

Alpheus Williams, a NINS graduate, was a somewhat eccentric but well-liked mathematics professor who was affectionately known as A-squared Williams. Professor William's life story is typical of students and faculty at the NINS during its early years. He was born on May 19, 1870, in Canton, Illinois. At the age of 14 he began the study of short-hand with a teacher near his home. In 1890 he came to Valparaiso to study in the commercial program and worked as an assistant instructor while completing advanced courses. After graduating from the Commercial Course in 1891 he continued to teach in the department while studying part-time to earn Bachelor of Arts and Bachelor of Science degrees. In 1895 he resigned his position at Valparaiso and with two associates founded a normal school in Bloomfield, Iowa. He served as

The year 1907 marks the genesis of engineering as an organizationally independent program. In that year Civil Engineering was separated from the Scientific Department. In the previous year it had been listed as one of five divisions of the Scientific Department along with Higher Mathematics, Laboratories, Natural Science, and Biology. Higher Mathematics included courses in astronomy, plane surveying, and mechanical drawing, while Natural Science included chemistry, physics and physiology. In 1907, 83 students who had been in the Civil Engineering division in 1906 were reclassified as being in the Civil Engineering Department, and their names were listed separately in the catalog for the first time.

Reflecting a move toward a more traditional curriculum, the 1908 catalog listed a detailed two-year curriculum in preparation for courses in Civil Engineering. It included the usual courses in mathematics, physics, chemistry, mechanical drawing, descriptive geometry, English, German history, and a whole year of wood shop work from bench to pattern making and foundry. This concept survived only one year. In 1909 a significantly revised curriculum for the full 12 quarters was instituted, the major change being a reduction of the amount of shop work. This new curriculum coincided with the arrival in 1909 of Ray Cyrus Yeoman as Professor of Civil Engineering. Professor Yeoman had graduated from Purdue in 1907 with a B.S.C.E. and in 1909 with a C.E. degree.

---

president of this school until 1902, when he returned to Valparaiso as a professor of mathematics. In 1904 he took a leave for post-graduate work in engineering at the University of Illinois. On his return from this year, plans for the new civil engineering program were set in motion. There is no direct evidence that this leave was part of a plan to develop the engineering program, but President Brown had helped to finance the graduate education of other promising teachers. In 1920, Valparaiso University honored Williams with the degree of Doctor of Science. In 1922, he became the vice president, treasurer, and business manager of the university. The following year he was the Dean of the College of Arts and Sciences. He resigned in 1927 and retired to tend his ten-acre apple orchard behind his home at the northeast corner of Lincolnway and Roosevelt. He died in 1940. Of interest to engineers is the fact that his brother, Dr. Clement Williams, a civil engineering professor, was president of Lehigh University from 1935 to 1942.

The new civil engineering program awarded the graduate with the degree of Civil Engineer, one typically earned after completing a Bachelor of Science in Civil Engineering. Fifteen Civil Engineer degrees were awarded to the first engineering class in 1909. Even though the Valparaiso catalog contained no reference to earning the Bachelor's degree, the 1910 graduation program listed four Civil Engineer and 12 Bachelor of Civil Engineering degrees. The Bachelor's degree was earned after eight quarters of study and the Civil Engineer degree was awarded after students had taken four additional quarters of professional courses. Many students concluded their work with the Bachelor's degree. The 1911 commencement program listed one candidate for the Master of Science in Civil Engineering.

Classroom time requirements were listed as Recitation or Lecture, Laboratory or Shop, Drawing, and Field. Based on converting the required hours into the current system of credits in which a lecture or recitation hour is one credit hour and three hours of lab work is worth one credit hour, the Civil Engineer degree required 278 quarter credits or 185 semester credits. In the first year, the required time in classes and labs averaged 38.5 hours. The final two years averaged 27 hours. The first two years required 128 credits. The third year was primarily civil engineering courses and required 57 credits. (Nationally, current programs require between 125 and 135 credit hours for a B.S. degree.) These 185 credit hours were distributed (to the nearest credit hour) as follows:

Mathematics	25	English	7	Surveying	17	Commercial Law	3
Chemistry	13	German	20	Geology	7	Bacteriology	1
Phys. & Astr.	21	Drawing	12	Shop	2	Civil Engr.	57

Ray Cyrus Yeoman

This new civil engineering curriculum coincided with the arrival in 1909 of Ray Yeoman at Valparaiso as Professor of Civil Engineering. A small biography of him in a 1915 edition of *The Torch* credits him with introducing this "up-do-date system of programs for class organization." Professor Yeoman was born on July 27, 1883, at Pleasant Ridge, a small farming community 3 miles east of

Courses in Mathematics ranged from Solid Geometry to Differential Equations.

The Civil Engineering courses were:

Engineering Materials	Applied Mechanics	Bridge Design	Bridges, Harbors, and Canals
Roads and Pavements	Static Mechanics	Steel Frame Buildings	Concrete
Municipal Engineering	Hydrology	Water Supply	Stereotomy (stone shaping)
Railway Construction	Theory of Framed Structures	Structures	Design Lab Test Lab

In each year after 1909 adjustments to the civil engineering curriculum were made. By 1915 the 20 credits of German had been removed, and small reductions in other areas made, in favor of adding more engineering courses, such as mechanical engineering oriented courses in Heating and Ventilating, Engines and Boilers, and Gas Power. Credits in engineering increased from 57 to 76.

Valparaiso University quickly attained a world-wide reputation as a school where a motivated student of any age and academic background could get a Civil Engineering degree for the lowest cost in the shortest time. As the 1910 catalog stated, "It has been, and will continue to be, the purpose of the school to accommodate itself to the students rather than to compel them to accommodate themselves to it." Domestic students came from locations as diverse as New York City, Los Angeles, Montana, Iowa, and South Carolina. Of the approximately 280 students enrolled in 1914-1915, 29 were from foreign countries: Canada (6); Bulgaria (4);

> Rensselaer in Jasper County, Indiana. He completed high school in Rensselaer in 1902. After teaching school for a year he enrolled at Purdue and earned the B. S. C. E. in 1907. He stayed on at Purdue as an assistant instructor and was awarded the C. E. degree in 1909. In 1911 upon the untimely death of Professor Bogarte, Professor Yeoman took charge of the engineering department as dean. He remained at Valparaiso until 1917 when he left in mid year to teach at Purdue. Information about his career after he left Valparaiso has not been found, but he died in 1962 in Indianapolis and is buried in Rensselaer.

Philippines (3); Japan, Russia, and India (2 each); Turkey, England, Ireland, Chile, Assyria, Poland, Peru, Cuba, Brazil, and China (1 each). The graduating class of 1915 also included the first two women engineering graduates, sisters (probably twins) Ethel and Merle McCall of Veroqua, Wisconsin. They had previously graduated with Bachelor of Pedagogy degrees from Valparaiso. There is no record of what they did with their engineering degrees after graduation.

ADDITIONAL DEGREE PROGRAMS ARE ADDED AND PLANNED

Enrollment grew rapidly, reaching a peak in 1914 with 288 in civil engineering and 4477 in the entire university. The largest number of graduates was in 1915 when 17 Bachelor of Civil Engineering and 33 Civil Engineer degrees were awarded. A study done at the time found that graduation rates across the nation were no more than 40%. Enrollment data for the period is reasonably detailed, but it does not lend itself to an accurate calculation of the Valparaiso graduation rate. A rough estimate is that it may have been as low as 25%, a rate closer to that of the late 19th century. Valparaiso's open admission policy, lack of prerequisites, and high standards were the most likely causes of the high failure rate.

In 1913 the civil engineering department was renamed the engineering department and Professor David Snader joined the faculty to develop an architectural engineering degree program. The 1914-15 catalog presented a complete description of the three-year program in architectural engineering, the Valparaiso equivalent of the typical four-year program.

FRANK R. THEROUX
Frank Theroux was born on January 27, 1891, in New Haven, Connecticut, and attended grade and high school in Springfield, Massachusetts. According to the February, 1922, *Who's Who in Valpo* publication, at the age of 18 he began work as a mining engineer in California and Arizona. With this experience he decided that he would profit from a technical

It drew heavily on the existing strengths of the civil engineering and the fine arts programs. By any measure, the class requirements were brutal: many quarters required 18-20 hours of attendance at recitations and another 20 or more in studio or lab work each week. This curriculum appeared in each catalog through 1917-18 and, without comment, disappeared from the 1918-1919 catalog. The 1918 college yearbook, *The Record*, contains a picture of the architectural engineering class, which shows eight men and one woman. One degree was awarded in 1918 to A. J. Whitlaw of Buenos Aires, Argentina. Apparently the course failed to attract or retain sufficient students to make it viable after the collapse of enrollment that occurred when the country entered the war in Europe.

The 1914-1915 catalog also announced new programs in mechanical, electrical, and chemical engineering. The civil and architectural programs were described as being "fully developed" with the rest being "carried through the first year." To align the organization of the University with current American academic practice, a Department of Arts and Sciences was organized in 1916, and in 1917 the Departments of Engineering, Pharmacy, Law, and Arts and Sciences were renamed as Schools. There is no evidence that this decision changed anything more than terminology.

The statement about mechanical, electrical, and chemical engineering programs occurred in every catalog through 1918-1919, with no evidence of any attempt to extend them beyond the first year. The 1919-1920 catalog lists Chemical Engineering as fully developed but does not describe the course requirements. The commencement programs of May and August, 1920, list 24 Bachelor's degrees in civil engineering and three in chemical engineering.

---

education and enrolled at Valparaiso in 1912. As an experienced surveyor, he taught surveying to support himself while a student and graduated with the Civil Engineer professional degree in 1915. Following graduation he returned to the east and worked in railroad construction and land surveying. Evidently his work at Valparaiso had been impressive, for he was only 25 years old when he was called back to lead the engineering program as dean in December, 1917. He died in 1978.

What did the administration intend by continually announcing programs that it failed to offer? Did it ever intend to add the second and third years, or was engineering simply the loser in the yearly competition for limited funds for the necessary capital and personnel additions? New programs in mechanical and electrical engineering were going to require investment in laboratory equipment and space. Significant resources for a building and staff had been allocated to start the domestic science course in 1914. Perhaps that project had cost more than expected. Had there been serious intentions to offer complete courses, statements that a second year would be offered in the next academic year would have appeared in the catalogs. None did. There is no answer to this puzzle.

Faculty and Classrooms

It has not been possible to determine accurately who taught the engineering courses. The catalogs in these years apparently listed faculty titles based on what the teacher did when first joining the faculty. For instance, many sources indicate that Professor Bogarte originated and for many years led the elocution program and later became dean of the engineering program, yet the catalogs list him only as Professor of Higher Mathematics. Professor Williams, another engineering instructor, also was identified only as Professor of Mathematics. In addition to Professor Yeoman, the 1909 catalog listed H. Lowry as Professor of Railway Engineering. Apparently he left after only one year and was not replaced. Assistants in surveying or civil engineering are also named. Attendance and graduation lists show that many of these assistants were advanced students who, having come to the university with practical experience that qualified them to assist in teaching, were working their way through college.

After the death of Dean Bogarte in 1911, Professor Yeoman served as dean until 1917. A student publication reported that he had taken a leave that summer, and the students were not sure he would return. During the summer Frank R. Theroux, a graduate of 1915, returned to the campus to take on Dean Yeoman's responsibilities. To the students' relief, Dean Yeoman returned for the fall term; however, he did leave in December to take a position at Purdue. After having left again at the start of the fall term, Theroux returned permanently as dean in December and held the position until 1923.

It has been even more difficult to identify the locations of designated engineering classrooms. The following inferences are made from photographs and comments in various publications in the university archive. In the early years classrooms were most certainly in the Old College Building since it was the only general classroom building. The core of the engineering course was surveying, requiring only the great outdoors and a room to store the instruments. The drawing work was probably done in the same quarters as those used for other drawing courses offered as part of the fine arts programs. In 1879-80 the L-shaped Commercial Hall was constructed at the southwest corner of College and Union Streets as a combination classroom and residence hall. The third floor housed the classrooms for the commercial courses in one wing and for the fine arts courses in the other wing. Most likely the drawing work was done there. Information about the manual training course established at the turn of the century indicated that its shop area occupied the south wing of the first floor of Commercial

Material Testing Lab - 1912

Hall. A drafting room was soon thereafter installed in the west wing. These areas had originally been a dining hall and kitchen. Some time after Commercial Hall was built, a brick building, later to be known as Foundry Annex, and a boiler plant were constructed west of the south wing and adjacent to the west wing. While no direct evidence has been found, it is reasonable to assume that the manual training courses and the engineering courses made use of the same shop, drafting, and foundry facilities. The only other specialized area needed for civil engineering was for testing materials. While there is no clear written evidence of this fact, it would have been natural for Professor Bogarte to use his bookstore building for engineering classes. A universal testing machine which figures prominently in many photos from the period is clearly in the basement of a building with basement windows that look like those of the Bogarte Bookstore building.

In the late teens, Dean Theroux wrote in the engineering portion of the yearbook about his hopes to find a new home for the Engineering Department in the Medical Building after the medical school had been closed. Sometime in the early twenties this move did happen. A special *Engineering Bulletin* for 1924-25 contains a picture of the Science and Medical buildings (Baldwin and Heimlich Halls), identifying them as the School of Pharmacy and the School of Engineering. Another photo taken from the railroad side of the buildings shows PHARMACY and ENGINEERING painted on the friezes at the top of the buildings. According to the bulletin, facilities for the School of Engineering were General Drafting Room, Structural Drafting Room, Materials Testing Laboratory, Woodworking Shop, Machine Shop, three Chemistry Laboratories, two Physics Laboratories, and Surveying Room. Moreover, "The equipment of this department is sufficient to handle every need of the student in surveying, testing, and steam engine study. Thirty complete sets of surveying instruments and drafting machines are available for student use." The bulletin also made special note of two universal testing machines. These two machines made the move to the new Engineering Laboratory in 1949 and one lasted well into the Gellersen Center years. In its last years it was an outdoor sculpture on the east side of Gellersen.

STUDENT ACTIVITIES

Dean Bogarte, Professor Yeoman, and Professor Williams provided several excellent opportunities for student professional development. In 1909 Professor Yeoman established a student Civil Engineering Society. The first edition of the *Engineering Annual*, published by the Civil Engineering Department in May, 1911, contained professional articles prepared by the faculty and selected students. Even after Professor Bogarte's untimely death in 1911, it was published for at least five more years under the direction of Dean Yeoman. Only the first edition survives in the university archive. The titles of the articles in the first edition reflect the quality of work being done by both faculty and students. The student work was undoubtedly the fruit of the thesis course required of candidates for the C.E. degree. Articles written by the faculty in the first edition were the following: "The Fourth Dimension" by Professor Bogarte, "Concrete Forms" by Professor Yeoman, and "The Origin of the Earth" by Lee F. Bennett, Professor of Geology and Mineralogy. Student written articles were: "An Example of Slow Burning Construction," "Design of Railway Plate Deck Girder Bridge," "Design of Steel Standpipe," "Investigation of the Strength of Nailed Joints" (with a picture of a nailed joint being tested in a universal test machine), and "Pratt Truss Railway Bridge."

In 1916 Professor Yeoman formed a student professional society called the American Association of Engineers, using the same name as an organization that had been established by practicing engineers in Chicago a year earlier. The student society was very proud of the fact that it received the second charter when the national organization decided to recognize student groups in 1918. At biweekly local chapter meetings, practicing engineers made presentations on current engineering topics. Engineering sections of several of the yearbooks of the era commented about the importance of this organization in the professional development of students.

The End of an Era

An observer of Valparaiso University in 1912 would have seen an experiment in education that had been successful almost beyond any reasonable expectation. Graduates from the early days had distinguished themselves in various fields, and Henry B. Brown was recognized as a national figure in higher education. Enrollment was still rising toward its peak in 1914 of nearly 5000 students on campus and at the medical and dental schools in Chicago. New programs were still being added. Architectural, electrical, mechanical, and chemical engineering were announced in 1913. In 1914, a high school department and a domestic science department, housed in the newly completed Domestic Science Building (later called Arts-Law and still later called DeMotte) were announced. In 1915 a department of agriculture was established, and a year later a school of Bible studies was started.

However, in 1912, the first of several events occurred that brought Valparaiso University to the brink of collapse. In Boston to receive the 33rd degree of the Masonic order, President Brown had a stroke that, while not fatal, prevented his active management of the university. President Brown was 65 at the time of his stroke, and Vice President Oliver Perry Kinsey only two years younger. As events unfolded, it is clear that while Brown and Kinsey had considered plans for the future of Valparaiso University after their active involvement ended, they had failed to complete them. Valparaiso was a joint proprietorship, the Brown and Kinsey partnership owning most of the property and assets and the Brown family owning the rest outright. They intended to convert the university to a more typical non-profit institution with a self perpetuating board of directors. While they had other financial resources, their primary source of wealth was Valparaiso University itself. Their vision was that this new organization would go into effect when the organization had acquired the financial resources necessary to buy the firm of Brown and Kinsey. None of their plans had been initiated when President Brown had his stroke.

When it became apparent that President Brown would not be able to continue active management, his wife Neva called on their son Henry

Kinsey Brown, then 22 years old, to return home and help manage what was their family business. Apparently convinced that the plan to convert the control of the institution was not wise, she wanted to continue Valparaiso University as a family business and blocked efforts toward the conversion. Vice President Kinsey took over as president, although he would only accept the title of Acting President in deference to his old friend. Henry Kinsey Brown became Treasurer. As he became involved in the business, he became convinced that the days of the "Poor Man's Harvard" were ending and that the university would have to move toward the mainstream to survive. His vision clashed with President Kinsey's view that the old ways had served them well and should be continued.

Engineering Society - 1916

The second precipitating event was the outbreak of war in Europe in 1914. Its immediate effect on the institution was minimal, only some loss of foreign students, especially from Eastern Europe. By 1916, though, domestic students began to leave to take jobs in industry as it geared up to supply the war effort in Europe. But the entry of the United States into the war in April, 1917, set in motion events that led to the near collapse of the institution. During that year it is estimated that more than 1300 students were drafted or left to work in war industries. And new students failed to arrive. Dean Yeoman reported that engineering enrollment had declined by 50%. In late 1917, President Brown died and O. P. Kinsey was named president. To make a bad year even worse, fire destroyed two dormitories. Faced with a debt from the construction of the Domestic Science Building and the need for investment to maintain accreditation of the Medical College, the administration sold the Medical College to Loyola University.

But the business continued to accumulate debt. Only one and a half years later, President Kinsey, approaching the age of 70, announced the dissolution of the firm of Brown and Kinsey and his retirement. The terms of the dissolution were never made public, but apparently Kinsey ceded his interest in the partnership in a manner that transferred all of its debt to the Brown family and freed Kinsey from all financial relationships to Valparaiso University. President Kinsey retired to Florida, and in 1919 Henry K. Brown, not yet 29 years old, became president. In one short year he determined that he was not suited to be a university president. In July, 1920, he announced the creation of the Board of Directors that had been envisioned by his father, resigned his presidency, and announced that the board had appointed Daniel R. Hodgdon as president. At the time many viewed him as a front man for the Brown family, one who provided the path for the family to liquidate its holdings. As it turned out, his one-year presidency was a disaster.

This chain of events, starting with the incapacitation of President Brown in 1912, goes a long way to explain the failure of the engineering program to expand beyond its civil engineering roots. Enrollment began to decline already in 1916, and debt began to rise. It may be that a simple lack of money to develop the laboratories for electrical and mechanical engineering prevented the expansion of the School of Engineering. Nor would Brown and Kinsey have given up on their medical school dream and sold their medical school in Chicago if there had been any other way to keep their university afloat.

The Engineering Profession Looks at the Education of an Engineer

It took until 1918 to publish the report of the study of engineering education first proposed in 1907 by the Society for the Promotion of Engineering

Education (SPEE). It was published as Bulletin 11 of the Carnegie Foundation for the Advancement of Teaching and titled "A Study of Engineering Education Prepared for the Joint Committee on Engineering Education of the National Engineering Societies." After working on the project for several years after 1907 and acquiring a considerable amount of data, the committee realized that it needed a full-time expert to bring the data together. In 1915 it turned to the Carnegie Foundation who employed Professor Charles Mann of the University of Chicago to complete the study and write the report. In engineering education literature this report is usually called the Mann Report rather than by its formal name.

The 100 page report is presented in three sections: Present Conditions, The Problems of Engineering Education, and Suggested Solutions. Mann made on-campus visits to 20 colleges, primarily in the East and Upper Midwest. Two aspects of the report stand out: 1) the significant effort to obtain as much numerical data as possible in order to define the problems and 2) the many examples of what would today be called "best practices." Engineering educators will perhaps not be surprised that many of the identified problems still exist 90 years later.

One problem that today has been ameliorated but not solved is the dropout rate. The apocryphal professor of a freshman course who years ago told his students to "look to your left and right; only one of you will graduate" was not too far wrong. The estimated average for retention in the Mann Report in 1918 was 40% with a range of 25% to 50%. It is better now, but not by a lot. Lax admission standards were cited as one reason for poor retention. Since many beginners had no real knack for engineering, entrance exams matched to the engineering curriculum were called for. A second reason given in the Mann Report was that the first two years contained little or no engineering work to inspire students who did have the talent. The report recommended real engineering projects in the first two years.

A recurring theme throughout the report was that the upper division courses failed to give sufficient attention to some of the non-technical knowledge necessary for a successful engineering career. For example, they contained instruction in the theory of design but gave little consideration to the problems of "labor, organization, values and costs." A study of 168 new hires at General Electric in 1913 found only slight correlation between college grades and the work performance ratings by supervisors. Also, the role and amount of shopwork in the curriculum was considered but no definite recommendations were made. Cooperative education, as pioneered by the University of Cincinnati, was recommended as a partial solution for the problem of providing industry-oriented practical training. The curriculum was also faulted for having too many courses and too much subject material. For pedagogical reasons the report recommended no more than 16-18 credits per semester instead of the more typical 20-24 and five courses at most per semester. Progress has been made in this area; most programs now average 16-17 credits per semester.

More emphasis on humanities in the curriculum was also recommended; however, foreign languages were not recommended since they emphasized only grammar and vocabulary. Professional engineers surveyed were nearly unanimous in supporting the elimination of foreign language from the college curriculum. They felt that it was appropriate only in high school. Another interesting recommendation that is still made today was that colleges should teach young faculty and teaching assistants how to teach.

Subsequent events make it hard to determine the impact of the Mann Report. It came out just at the height of the disruptions caused by World War I and evidently was widely ignored. Just four years later, a second study was launched by SPEE, one that would be even more extensive by a factor of 10 to 1, based on the number of pages in the final report.

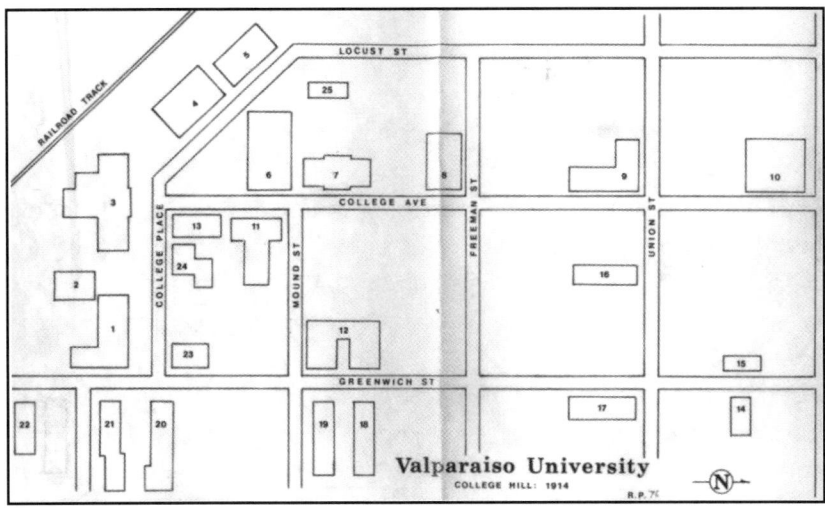

Campus Map - 1914

CLASSROOM BUILDINGS

3 Old College
4 Science/Baldwin
5 Medical/Biology/Heimlich
6 Auditorium/Chapel
7 Flint/Library/Heritage
8 Domestic Science/Arts-Law/ DeMotte
9 Commercial/Engineering/ Benton
11 Music/Kinsey
13 Bogarte Bookstore/Bogarte

RESIDENTIAL BUILDINGS

1 East
2 South
10 Altruria
12 Lembke
14 Corboy
15 New Meade
16 Monandnock
17 Stiles
18 Columbia
19 Mound
20 Eiss
21 Vinyard
22 Union
23 Windsor Locksley
24 YMCA
25 Livingston

FOUR

IN SEARCH OF NEW IDENTITIES: 1919-1930

The decade known in America as the "Roaring Twenties" was anything but roaring for Valparaiso University and its engineering program. For both, it was spent finding and solidifying new identities. With the passing of Henry Baker Brown and the retirement Oliver Perry Kinsey, Valparaiso University ended 46 years of prominence as a unique institution in American higher education. In 1919, Henry Kinsey Brown, the son of Henry Baker Brown, assumed the presidency. Almost two generations younger than his father and President Kinsey, he was convinced that the educational model that had brought Valparaiso to prominence had run its course, and the university's survival lay in moving it to a mission similar to that of other private universities. Very quickly the campus community, both faculty and students, split into two factions. One faction embraced his proposals and the other demanded a return to the old ways. Ultimately his leadership did not survive this factionalism, and Valparaiso University nearly did not.

THE POST-BROWN-KINSEY ERA BEGINS

Upon assuming the presidency, Henry K. Brown enacted the transition plan for control of the university that his father and Kinsey had proposed. Even though his initial attempts to find benefactors or purchasers did not succeed, in June of 1920 he created a board of directors consisting of prominent local businessmen and industrialists from Chicago and New York, vesting this board with official control of the university. With this organization he hoped to secure individuals to endow the university so that eventually the new organization could buy the Brown family's ownership of the property. Keenly aware that he was not an educator, he quickly began a search for someone to assume the academic leadership of the university. Early in the summer of 1920 Daniel R. Hodgdon, A.B., M.A., M.S., Sc.D., LL.D., M.D., Ph.D. assumed the position of dean of the faculty. He had a reputation as an able administrator and had most recently been president of Hanneman Medical College in Philadelphia. As soon as the new board of directors was organized in July, 1920, Henry Kinsey Brown resigned his presidency and the board appointed Daniel Hodgdon to replace him. Brown returned to his position as the business manager of the university.

President Hodgdon immediately continued the fund-raising and systemic changes that Henry K. Brown had started. He announced new plans with regularity and fanfare and presented an educational flowchart that would be the pride of any management consultant. Enrollment picked up for the fall term and for a few months the campus optimism returned; but soon the factionalism between supporters of the status quo and supporters of change returned. Histories written by Richard Baepler and John Strietelmeier examine this unpleasant time in the university's history in great detail. The short story is that some student leaders who did not favor the changes documented that President Hodgdon's only degree of substance in the long list of degrees behind his name was the A.B. The rest had either been granted or merely claimed for a minimal amount or sometimes for no academic work at all. Even before this information became public, in January, 1921, Henry Kinsey Brown resigned his position and severed all active relationships with Valparaiso University. The following April, the executive committee of the new board of directors dismissed President Hodgdon from office. John Roessler, an early graduate of Brown's school and a long-time respected professor of German and Mathematics, put off his retirement and assumed the presidency.

The College of Applied Science – a Grand Plan for Engineering

The vision of President H. K. Brown for the new Valparaiso University included the expansion of the engineering program to take advantage of the rapid industrialization that was occurring on the lakeshore in neighboring Lake County. The city of Gary had been established only 13 years earlier by United States Steel to house workers in its massive integrated steel mill. Standard Oil had built a refinery in Whiting; Inland

Steel and Youngstown Sheet and Tube soon followed. The Calumet Region was growing rapidly as these companies generated related industries.

In every year following 1914, course catalogs described mechanical, electrical, and chemical engineering as being offered but "not fully developed, being carried only through the first year." In the accelerated Valparaiso curriculum, the first year was, in fact, the general engineering half of a Bachelor of Science degree program. Coincident with the start of the presidency of Henry K. Brown in the fall of 1919, Charles Carroll Brown joined the engineering faculty. The following year a College of Applied Sciences was formed with him as its dean. It contained two divisions: the School of Engineering, which contained civil and architectural engineering and was headed by Frank Theroux, now as director instead of dean; and the School of Co-Industrial Engineering which contained programs in mechanical, electrical, and chemical engineering. The Co-Industrial Engineering curriculum was designed as a cooperative education experience. As the catalog put it, "The location of Valparaiso University in the midst of the great industrial district of Northwestern Indiana and Chicago is ideal for the co-ordination of study and practical experience outlined in the courses of study, at the same time that the city of Valparaiso itself is a quiet college town." For the first two years the student spent the summer quarters in industry and in the last two years, alternated quarters on campus and at work. While there is no direct evidence, it is likely that Professor Charles Brown developed and planned these new engineering programs during his first year at the university.

CHARLES CARROLL BROWN

Charles Brown was born at Austinburg, Ohio, on October 4, 1856. He attended Cornell University in 1874-75 and graduated with a C.E. degree from the University of Michigan in 1879. In 1883 he became one of the founding faculty members at Rose Polytechnic in Terre Haute and then from 1886 to 1893 he taught at Union College in Schenectady, New York, and served as its dean. In 1894 he relocated to Indianapolis where he served as City Engineer and then as editor of the magazine *Municipal Engineering*. While

The 1920-21 catalog described the programs in detail. The civil and architectural programs still met the requirements for the Civil Engineer or Architectural Engineer degree and could be completed in three calendar years or twelve quarters. The new chemical, electrical, and mechanical engineering degree programs required four calendar years, during which the student was in class only 10 quarters. Evidently the six quarters of industrial work did not receive any academic credit, since the earned degree was a Bachelor of Science. The professional Chemical Engineer, Electrical Engineer, or Mechanical Engineer degrees could be awarded by request upon two years of qualified industrial experience after graduation. This was a commonly accepted practice at the time.

The arrival of Professor Charles C. Brown as a member of the engineering faculty leads to an interesting speculation. Hiring a man of his age, 61, and experience was a complete departure from earlier practice. All of the previous appointments, including that of Dean Frank Theroux, were of young men with limited experience as engineers. Professor Brown came with a lifetime of experience and an outstanding record of performance as a teacher and engineer. Just how President Henry K. Brown recruited him to the faculty remains unknown. Why would a man with his experience, accomplishments, and age come to take over an engineering program at a school that he must have known was in financial trouble? It is tempting to suppose that he was a relative of the Brown family, but that fact has not been substantiated. All that can be said with certainty is that he was not a younger brother of Henry Baker Brown, as their biographies list different parents. They were, however, both from eastern Ohio. Soon after the departure of President Hodgdon

> editing that magazine he was instrumental in founding the organization that became the American Concrete Institute and published *Handbook for Cement Users*. He also served as secretary and president of the American Public Works Association. In 1913, the University of Michigan awarded him an honorary Master of Arts degree. In the year before he came to Valparaiso University he was with the Illinois Division of Highways. When he left Valparaiso, he took a position with the Department of Public Works of St. Petersburg, Florida. From 1927 to 1933 he was Professor of Civil Engineering at the University of Florida. He also served as president of the Florida chapter of the American Association of Engineers. He died November 26, 1949.

and the resignation of Henry K. Brown, Charles C. Brown also resigned. With him went the dreams for the five engineering degrees and the cooperative education program.

A More Modest School of Engineering

In the fall of 1921 the engineering organization reverted to a School of Engineering with "divisions of Civil, Electrical, and Mechanical Engineering." Frank Theroux was again Dean of Engineering. The catalog announced that since the electrical and mechanical courses had been first offered in 1920-21, only the first eight quarters would be offered in 1921-22. Even though the university enrollment continued to decline, no doubt abetted by the tumultuous events of the previous year and the ongoing attacks on the reputation of the school by the now-dismissed Hodgdon, plans for an enhanced engineering program were still being advanced. In the years immediately after World War I, the civil engineering course had been one of the more successful programs in attracting and retaining students. At the May, 1920, commencement, 102 degrees were awarded: 33 in the entire liberal arts areas; 48 in pharmacy and chemistry; 4 in law; and 19 in civil engineering. Adding electrical and mechanical engineering degree programs must have looked like a very viable way to increase enrollment.

However, the financial situation continued to worsen and the university lost its accreditation by the State of Indiana, making it much more difficult to attract students. It became infeasible to add the final year in the new EE and ME programs in 1922-23, but the catalog announced intentions to add them in 1923-24. The Civil Engineer degree was eliminated (the last being awarded in 1923), and only a B.S.C.E was offered. The new B.S.C.E. course required 210 quarter credits, equivalent to 140 semester credits, for graduation. All but the 9 credits in English were in math, science, engineering, and business law. Mathematics started at college algebra and finished at differential equations. Science consisted of chemistry, physics, and bacteriology. Engineering work included wood shop, descriptive geometry, railway curves and construction, surveying, stresses, roads and pavements, hydraulics,

Materials Testing Laboratory

bridge design, strength of materials, water supply, reinforced concrete, mechanics, testing materials, sewerage, masonry construction, structural design, heating and ventilating, heat engines, and engineering economics. By eliminating some science and reducing the content of some introductory courses, the old Civil Engineer degree course had been repackaged as a Bachelor of Science course with almost all the advanced courses in the Civil Engineer program still intact.

To make them correspond to typical curricula at other colleges, the electrical and mechanical curricula were significantly different from the civil program. In addition to the English courses, 10 semester credits of foreign language, 4 of public address, and 2 of English literature were listed. Mathematics and science were the same as in the civil course. Wood shop was augmented with pattern making and machine shop. Mechanical engineers had a course in mechanisms and the electrical engineers took a chemistry course in qualitative analysis. A total of 116 quarter credits, or 77 semester credits, of engineering were required. This number of credits was standard for the time.

Perhaps the elimination of the Civil Engineer degree was more than Frank Theroux could take; in the summer of 1922 he resigned his appointment as dean and left the university. Henry T. Fisher was named acting dean. In February, 1923, the Old College Building, the heart of the school of Brown and Kinsey, burned to the ground. The university was so short of funds that it could not even clear away the rubble. Whatever hope there had been to complete the EE and ME programs was now gone, and in 1923-24, a two year pre-engineering course that could be completed at other institutions was made permanent.

On January 1, 1923, Horace M. Evans became president of Valparaiso University, taking over from Milo J. Bowman, dean of the School of Law, who had served in that capacity for the six months after the retirement of President Roessler. The board presented him with the challenge of finding a buyer who could provide the capital to stabilize the finances of the university. Various fraternal and church organizations were approached without success, but the Indiana chapter of the Ku Klux Klan was interested. The Klan, officially a fraternal organization, was very active in Indiana political affairs during this period. It was essentially nativist, promoting anti-communism, anti-Catholicism, anti-Semitism, and white supremacy. At its peak in the early 20s, it claimed 15% of the male population of the country as members. Late in 1923, the Indiana chapter, without the authorization of the national organization, publicly indicated the Klan's interest in purchasing the university. However, the national organization quickly repudiated this overture. Unfortunately so many newspapers had reported the potential sale as an accomplished fact that for years to come many people believed that Valparaiso had become a Klan school. With the Klan out of the picture, President Evans and the Board turned to the State of Indiana. In early 1925, the Legislature approved a bill to purchase the university and establish it as the third normal school in the state. But Governor Ed Jackson vetoed the bill, ending that hope for saving Valparaiso University. With this setback many doubted that the university would be able to offer classes in the fall quarter of 1925.

Despite this deteriorating situation, the School of Engineering continued as best it could. After serving two years as acting dean, Henry T. Fisher officially became dean in the summer of 1924. The 1924-25 catalog announced that graduates who received the B.S.C.E degree could be awarded the Civil Engineer degree after two years of acceptable professional experience by presenting a satisfactory thesis on an approved subject. The two-year programs in electrical and mechanical engineering were coordinated with those of "standard engineering schools" and could be completed in six consecutive quarters or two years without the summer quarter. The catalog claimed that "arrangements have been perfected with other institutions whereby credit for two years' work will be allowed." Whether any engineering school would actually accept these credits from a school not accredited by the North Central Association of Colleges and Schools is not clear. There is no convenient source of information about the number of students who actually took the EE and ME two-year courses, but the CE course did not suffer too badly in enrollment. Whereas there were 15 graduates in 1918, there still were 9 in 1925.

Throughout the early 1920s, Valparaiso University also operated a vocational training program as part of a government program to teach practical skills to wounded and "shell-shocked" war veterans. It is hard to tell from the records which teachers were involved in the engineering program or the vocational program. Some were probably involved in both. The vocational programs included Mechanical Drawing, Machine Shop, Electric Shop, Shoe Shop, Automobile Shop, and Watch and Jewelry Repair. During the difficult economic times of the early 1920s, the income from these vocational programs contributed significantly to the overall budget of the university. When the the federal government terminated the program, the equipment, supplied and owned by the

HENRY TOWNSEND FISHER

Henry Fisher was born on Sept. 7, 1895, in Sioux City, Iowa. He entered Valparaiso as a freshman in the Civil Engineering course in 1915 and graduated with the C.E. degree in 1918. He joined the army and was commissioned a Second Lieutenant in the Field Artillery. At the conclusion of the war, he returned to Valparaiso for the 1919-1920 year as an assistant in mechanical drawing. He then spent one year each at Universal Portland Cement and Decatur Bridge Company before returning to Valparaiso in 1922. He served two years as acting dean before being appointed as dean. He resigned his position at the conclusion of the 1924-25 academic year. Nothing is known of his subsequent career.

federal government, was given to the university. The applicable equipment was later used to equip laboratories for the electrical and mechanical engineering labs. Moses W. Uban began his long teaching career at Valparaiso during this period. After teaching English during the 1922-23 year, because of his practical machine shop experience, he was recruited to teach the machine shop courses in the vocational program when an unexpected vacancy occurred. When the vocational training program was terminated, he began teaching the engineers.

A New Lutheran University

In the summer of 1925, despite the uncertainty of the early 1920s, Valparaiso University found its new identity. In a whirlwind of activity starting in the spring of 1925, a Lutheran University Association was incorporated and obtained financing to purchase the university, taking control of the assets of Valparaiso University on August 11, 1925. The purchase price was $176,500. This modest amount was possible only because the Valparaiso Chamber of Commerce had secured the cancellation of $331,000 of locally held debt. Valparaiso University was now an independent Lutheran university, affiliated with, but not controlled by, what is now known as the Lutheran Church – Missouri Synod. Richard Baepler's history of Valparaiso University, *Flame of Faith, Lamp of Learning*, contains much more detail on the events leading up to and following this purchase.

This new ownership had no immediate impact on the academic programs of the university; all that had been in place before the change remained so. Dr. Evans continued as president until January, 1926, when having achieved his objective of finding new ownership for the university, he resigned. Reverend John C. Baur, the Lutheran University Association's secretary and on-campus representative after the purchase, was named acting president. Under his direction the campus buildings and grounds were cleaned up in the fall of 1925, and the rubble from the burned-out Old College Building was removed. Certainly, these immediate physical changes gave new hope to both student body and faculty that better times were ahead. In June, 1926, Dr. William H. T.

Dau, a 62–year-old professor of dogmatics at Concordia Seminary, assumed the presidency.

The scholarly Dr. Dau, however, was unsuited to the daunting task of bringing a university back from near collapse while at the same time putting a Lutheran stamp on its character. In the summer of 1927 he took a leave to regain his strength and had not fully resumed his presidency when he resigned in June, 1929. His greatest accomplishment, achieving accreditation by the North Central Association, occurred in March, 1929. Accreditation was a critical factor in attracting a sufficient number of new students to make the university financially viable. He was succeeded in May, 1930, by Reverend Oscar C. Kreinheder, who had been closely associated with the Lutheran University Association since its founding.

The Department of Engineering

It would be a few more years before the School of Engineering would get its new identity and realize its objective of four-year programs in civil, electrical, and mechanical engineering. Under the new Lutheran ownership, the academic programs were reorganized in 1927 and the School of Engineering became the Department of Engineering. Planning for full programs in mechanical, electrical, and chemical engineering continued during this period of transition. In 1922 Ross Winship began teaching mechanical engineering subjects and in 1924 F. R. Martin became the electrical engineering instructor. No catalog for the 1925-26 year has survived, but other sources indicate that Dean Henry Fisher left in the summer of 1925 and was succeeded as dean by Howard D. Harvey. Little is known about Dean Harvey except that he was a graduate of Ohio Northern University, where he earned a B.S.C.E. in 1919 and the C. E. degree in 1922.

The 1926-27 catalog presented full four-year curricula of 12 quarters in civil, chemical, electrical, and mechanical engineering. In that year all four years were offered for civil engineering and the first three years for the rest. Evidently during that year offerings in chemical engineering

Medical/Biology/Heimlich Hall. Used by Engineering in the 1920s

were reconsidered, since, in the 1927-28 catalog, students interested in chemical engineering were directed to apply to the head of the Department of Chemistry. This is not too surprising, since general enrollment was low, and chemical engineering historically has attracted fewer students than the other programs. Of 635 undergraduates only 71 were enrolled in engineering, clearly not enough to support a chemical engineering course.

In 1927, the university switched to a semester system. For the most part, the curriculum of the previous year was repackaged into a semester program with a net reduction of about 10 credits, from 147 to 137-139 depending on the degree. The only apparent serious loss was differential equations, which may have been packaged into the calculus course. Judged by present standards, the degree programs were seriously deficient in humanities courses. Other than freshman English, none was required. Mathematics began with college algebra and concluded with integral calculus. Basic science included only chemistry and physics. All three programs required two shop courses, two drawing courses, a descriptive geometry course, a surveying course, and an engineering economics course. The basic engineering courses in electrical and mechanical engineering were common to both programs, as were principles of industrial organization and factory management.

In all three programs the rest of the courses in the major had names that are still recognizable in contemporary curricula. The only exception is the electrical machinery courses, which have virtually disappeared from electrical engineering programs. The CE program had two unrestricted electives, the EE three, and the ME one. Graduates were still eligible for the professional degrees, but these degrees now required the completion of an approved thesis and four years of professional experience.

The year 1927 also marked relocation of the facilities for engineering from the Medical Building to the Commerce Building at the corner of Union and College, which then was renamed the Engineering Building. The spaces on the first floor had been previously used by the manual training courses for shops and drafting rooms. In earlier years, a foundry and steam power plant had been added as a west wing to the building. Many later Valparaiso students will remember this space as "foundry annex classroom." The 1927 catalog described the Engineering Building as containing "extensive machine shops, electrical labs, woodworking shops, drafting rooms, testing laboratories, foundries, a modern power plant, etc." Some parts of this building continued in use for engineering activities until the completion of Graland Hall in 1956. This new curriculum and location coincided with the arrival of Harry E. Bilger as head of the Department of Engineering. After three years, he left in 1930. No information has been found about his career after Valparaiso.

The catalogs for 1927, 1928 and 1929 repeated the statement that the fourth year of EE and ME would be offered in the following year. However, graduation records for 1928 list Donald D. Mallory as receiving a B.S.M.E and Alton T. Medsger a B.S.E.E. These were the first graduates awarded these degrees by Valparaiso University. Evidently either the catalog language was incorrect or special arrangements had been made for these students. The fourth year of EE and ME courses seem to have been offered in 1929-30, as one B.S.E.E., one B.S.C.E., and two B.S.M.E. degrees were awarded at the 1930 graduation. In addition to the three degrees, the 1930 catalog included a fourth degree program in Commercial Engineering, which could be earned by substituting business courses for some of the EE or ME courses. This degree was not available to civil engineering students. Clearly, at the beginning of the

1930s, engineering at Valparaiso University was already pursuing its new identity.

THE ENGINEERING PROFESSIONS SEEKS AN IMPROVED IDENTITY

While Valparaiso University and the College of Engineering were developing their new identities, the engineering education establishment and the engineering profession itself were also searching for a better definition of what it meant to be an engineer. Two initiatives, begun in the mid teens, had significant impact on the profession by the 1930s. The American Association of Engineers was established in 1915 and "A Study of Engineering Education" (the Mann Report) was published by the Carnegie Foundation in 1918. The essential objective of each of these initiatives was to define the meaning and role of the engineer in American society. Neither produced answers in its time, and for many, now almost 100 years later, the answers are still to be found. Both were concerned with the impact of the rapid transformation of America from an 18th century agricultural to a 20th century industrial society. Within those 100 years the role of the engineer in civil society was transformed from a novel concept to an important component of the developing economy. Was engineering, this new profession, on a par in status with medicine, law, or theology? And if so, what kind of credentials should be required? Where in the spectrum of technological services required for the new industrial society did the engineer fit? These questions became more difficult as mechanical, electrical, and chemical engineering took on significant importance and moved the bulk of engineering employment away from sole practice and government toward industrial work.

HARRY EDMUND BILGER

A native of Curwensville, Pennsylvania, Harry Bilger earned a Bachelor of Philosophy from Bucknell in 1903, a B.S.C.E from the University of Missouri in 1907, an M.S. in 1915 and a C.E. in 1923 from Bucknell. He had extensive experience in the construction and maintenance of the Chicago and Alton Railroad and the Central Railroad of New Jersey. Before coming to Valparaiso, he

The American Association of Engineers

The American Association of Engineers was founded in 1915 in Chicago by a group of younger engineers employed by the City of Chicago who felt that the established professional engineering societies were not sufficiently concerned with the needs of those just starting out in their profession. In their view the established societies (which claimed only a small fraction of employed engineers) had become elitist Eastern organizations interested primarily in technical matters and dismissive of the employment needs of engineers. The AAE was organized to be a pan-engineering organization that promoted professional ethics and the social and material welfare of engineers. Its focus on young engineers included the establishment of student chapters on college campuses, the second of which was installed at Valparaiso University in 1917. By specifically rejecting technical publications, the AAE concentrated on the individual engineer and the conditions of his professional practice. In 1922 it began to promote the establishment and enforcement of state professional registration laws.

Its rise to prominence was rapid, reaching, in 1921, a membership of more than 26,000, primarily but not exclusively civil engineers. Its rise and decline can be traced to a single issue: the cause of the college-educated engineers employed by American railroads. During the war the railroads had been nationalized and wages frozen; in its aftermath, the AAE supported the efforts of these engineers, along with railroad labor unions, to regain an equitable wage during a period of post-war inflation. The willingness of the organization to work for better employment conditions brought rapid membership increases, especially

---

had various responsible positions in bridge and road design with the Illinois State Highway Department. No information about his career after he left Valparaiso is known. A 1929 Valparaiso University publication states, "Mr. Bilger is an enthusiastic booster of our Engineering Department. He is very emphatic in his contention that Valparaiso University is unusually well-equipped to carry on the work of his department. In fact, he states, the engineering equipment is today much better than that of some other recognized schools attended by a considerably larger number of students."

by younger engineers. However, membership declined again when, after serious debate, the organization rejected trade unionism for its members and deemphasized wage and working conditions. While the ideal of raising the social and economic status of engineers remained, the AAE sought other means for achieving this goal. In 1934 the AAE became the National Society of Professional Engineers, and state licensure became the primary means for engineers to achieve professional recognition. Today the NSPE leaves the process by which an aspiring engineer obtains the knowledge to qualify for professional registration to engineering educators and the technical professional societies.

The Founding of the Engineers' Council for Professional Development

Within a few years of the publication of the Mann Report, it was clear to engineering educators that an even more extensive analysis was in order. The outcome was monumental: a 1000 page report titled "Report of the Investigation of Engineering Education 1923-1928" prepared by SPEE under the direction of Professor William E. Wickenden. It is generally known as the Wickenden Report. Its purpose was to provide the data needed to develop a coordinated plan for technical education that would win the support of the public and advance the cause of engineers as professionals. One immediate outcome of the report was the formation of the Engineers' Council for Professional Development (ECPD).

The major concerns of the engineering community in the 1920s are nicely summarized in the four original objectives of ECPD: guidance, education, training, and recognition. Guidance involved supplying information to students. The Wickenden Report provided great detail about the engineering colleges' admission standards and poor retention statistics. Inadequate high school preparation, lax administration of good admission standards, and the student's own poor understanding of the objectives of engineering education were blamed for the high rate of early student failures at the colleges. The education objective was to be met by appraising engineering curricula and maintaining a list of accredited curricula. The SPEE study obtained extensive data about existing curricula and the opinions of professional societies and practicing engineers in order to identify best practices and develop consensus about an undergraduate education that would best serve the nation and the engineering profession. To meet the training objective, ECPD promoted and provided post-graduate professional development materials and opportunities.

Commercial/Engineering/Benton Building with Foundry Annex and Steam Plant

Almost 250 pages of the Wickenden Report were devoted to a comparative study and analysis of the European technical education systems. The authors described the greater social and professional status of French and German engineers as well as the clearly defined system of professional and sub-professional technical education established by official government actions in Europe. Lacking the prospect of equivalent government actions in America, the engineering profession, through ECPD, intended to foster a more uniform and better quality national system of engineering education that would raise the professional status and recognition of American engineers. Two paragraphs from the Wickenden Report clearly summarize the situation at the time and point to the intended outcome.

In no other country have the engineering schools been so free from outside domination. They owe little to statecraft other than the provision of means for their extension and support. They owe little to the organized engineering profession except the benefits of occasional criticism of their aims and methods. They owe little to the industries except an ever-widening field of employment for their graduates. To a striking degree, these schools have been left to work out their own destiny and fend for themselves. This has been both the source of strength and weakness. There has been complete freedom for educational experimentation and innovation which, when exercised, has justified itself abundantly through a number of major advances. On the other hand the leaving of all initiative to individual institutions, with no coordination of policy, has resulted in failure to work out a well-rounded national system of technical education in its several natural divisions.

The engineering school has remained largely a thing apart, a seat of individual effort and of individual discipline, and has not achieved in America as in Germany a large place in the strategy of social progress. Is this its destiny? No doubt the engineering school will long remain primarily a teaching institution and place for research for inquiring minds; enlightened and inspired individuals will be its most precious gift to society; but it is scarcely conceivable in an essentially technological civilization that the school of technical science should be content to remain wholly a transmitting medium, with only a minor share in the creation of knowledge and with little or no share in shaping social institutions.

These two paragraphs laid out the underlying philosophy used to establish the criteria for accreditation. Throughout the years some details of the criteria have been adjusted to respond to current conditions, but the emphasis continues to be coordination of national engineering education policy through a core curriculum, creation of knowledge, and fostering the social awareness of engineers. In 1936 ECPD invited colleges to submit their programs for review. It took two years for the volunteer evaluators to visit all schools that had requested accreditation. All were considered to have been accredited in 1936.

FIVE

Promise Meets Reality: 1930-1940

One might wonder what Valparaiso University and its College of Engineering would look like today had the school in its new Lutheran identity had a chance to stabilize its finances and reputation before meeting head-on the Great Depression of the 1930s. While other Lutheran synods had long-established colleges for the education of both lay people and professional church workers, none had ever ventured into engineering education. With the basic educational reorganization from the Brown-Kinsey model completed, the new Lutheran administration resolved to establish a full engineering college separate from the arts and sciences college. Valparaiso was thus staking a claim to leadership in providing educational opportunities for Lutheran students in a profession clearly becoming more important in the economic life of the nation. While it is clear that the Board and the President understood the emerging importance of engineering, it is not so clear that they knew what they were getting into or what it would take to succeed. In the end, the reality of the extended economic depression coupled with the heavy financial commitment required for a quality engineering school resulted in the decision to close the college in 1939 and replace it with a department that offered a two year pre-engineering course articulated with the degree requirements of Purdue University.

During the 1930s the engineering community made significant strides to achieve greater professional recognition. As a result of the Wickenden Report, the Engineering Council for Professional Development was established, and in 1936 it organized a process to accredit college engineering programs. Almost immediately concerns were raised that four years of study were not sufficient to master the required body of knowledge, and thus to achieve the kind of professional standing accorded to graduates in Law and Medicine. A follow-up study completed in 1940 concluded that the nation would be best served if schools maintained the four-year plan, since there were no educational alternatives for those whose careers would not require a professional degree.

THE RETURN OF THE COLLEGE OF ENGINEERING

The decade of the thirties began with the appointment of Dr. Howard Wilson Moody as Head of the Department of Engineering. In Professor Moody, Valparaiso had found an experienced engineering educator for its leader. For a number of years the faculty and leadership at Valparaiso had been composed of young men who were long on energy but somewhat short on experience, but Professor Moody had a physics Ph.D. from the University of Chicago and had most recently been Dean of Engineering at Mississippi Agricultural and Mechanical College. The degree of optimism at the beginning of the decade is reflected in the actions taken by the board of directors at its October, 1930, meeting. On the recommendation of President Oscar C. Kreinheder, who had succeeded President Dau earlier in 1930, the board resolved to establish a College of Engineering consisting of these departments: Chemical Engineering and Metallurgy, Civil Engineering, Drawing and Architecture, Electrical Engineering, Mechanical Engineering, and Industrial Arts. By the time the planning had been completed, some changes had been made to the original proposal. Commercial engineering, which was not in the original proposal, was added as a degree option, the Chemical and Metallurgy department was reduced to Chemical, and Drawing and Architecture was dropped. The new college was launched with a celebratory dinner in March, 1931, at which a letter of congratulations from President Hoover was read. The fall semester of 1931 began with 101 students in the College of Engineering under the direction of Dean Moody.

In 1932 metallurgical and aeronautical programs were announced. These two essentially comprised the mechanical program for the first three years and required transfer to another college for completion. In 1933 the industrial arts program, which had been in existence since 1904 to train secondary school teachers and had been made the responsibility of the College of Engineering, was eliminated. Also in 1933, the chemical program was reduced to a two-year course which required transfer to another college for completion.

The commercial engineering course was slightly revised to eliminate the 1930 reference to exclusive enrollment for EE and ME students. It consisted of core courses in basic engineering and two each of CE, EE, and ME introductory courses, the rest of the advanced courses being replaced with 15 business courses. Both the Mann Report of 1918 and the Wickenden Report of 1928 gave significant attention to the growing importance of business concerns in the practice of engineering and the attendant need for the engineering curriculum to reflect this importance. It can be assumed that Dean Moody supported this commercial engineering course in response to the Wickenden Report. He would have been familiar with the recommendations of the report, since he was listed as the representative of Mississippi A&M in its creation.

Paul A. Cushman, a second experienced educator and a 1911 MIT graduate with a Sc.D. from Michigan joined the faculty in 1934. He had been on the Michigan faculty and had previously taught at the Polytechnic Institute of Brooklyn. Faculty reductions at Michigan due to the depression-induced enrollment declines made him available to Valparaiso. For the rest of the decade these two and four younger men with more modest academic accomplishments constituted the faculty. Because of the economic hard times and lack of broader opportunities, Valparaiso was able to attract and keep an engineering faculty with good qualifications.

HOWARD WILSON MOODY
Dr. Howard Moody was born on Oct. 24, 1876, in Dysart, Iowa. After graduating from the local high school, he attended the Tilford Collegiate Academy at Vinton, Iowa, and then Cornell College at Mount Vernon, Iowa, where he earned a B. A. degree in 1902. He taught in several high schools in Iowa; probably some of this teaching experience came before he finished his undergraduate work, a common situation since teachers with college degrees were the exception rather than the rule at this time. While at Cornell he was elected to Phi Beta Kappa. Some time later he began graduate work in pysics at the University of Chicago

Concerns About the Viability of the College

But the hopes for the college that were so high in 1931 soon met the reality of the Great Depression. Although times were already hard, every one was expecting a quick return to prosperity. The economy did not recover. By 1934, engineering enrollment had declined from 101 to 50. Total university enrollment declined from 627 to 446 in 1935. In 1933 President Kreinheder established a curriculum and educational planning committee with the following members: President Kreinheder, Dean of the Faculty Frederick W. Kroencke, Registrar and Business Manager Albert Scribner, and Professor Walther Miller. In his January, 1935, report to the board President Kreinheder made several points. The committee had spent considerable time in the past months on the problem of enrollment in the College of Engineering. For the previous three years he had called attention to the decrease in engineering enrollment and had warned that something would have to be done if the situation did not improve. The enrollment had declined to 43. (The catalog for 1934-35, however, listed 50 engineering students) The committee had considered reducing the offerings in engineering from four to two years, giving the following reasons: "(1) the saving in salaries of at least three instructors; (2) the use of the money for the expansion of other departments for which there may be greater demand; (3) the fact that the last two years now being offered in engineering are not fully accredited by all engineering colleges; (4) the difficulty of competing with big engineering schools such as Purdue in our own immediate vicinity." But after the committee had consulted with the head of public relations and another

---

(studying with Nobel Prize winners Robert Millikan and Albert Michelson), and was awarded the Ph.D. in 1912. His dissertation, published in both English and German, was titled *Specific Heats of Air and Carbon Dioxide*. After holding teaching positions for a short time at Lafayette College and Williams College, he joined the faculty of Mississippi Agricultural and Mechanical College (now Mississippi State University) as head of its physics department. In 1925 he was appointed Dean of the College of Engineering at Mississippi A&M but was relieved of his position in 1930 after being on the losing side of a Mississippi political battle. He began his service at Valparaiso in 1930. In 1942, at the age of 65, he relinquished his administrative responsibilities but remained an active faculty member at Valparaiso until his death on March 24, 1949.

representative of the faculty, "the committee resolved unanimously to continue the four-year course for at least another year." The reasons given for this conclusion were: "(1) the loss of prestige in the field; (2) the loss of not only the Seniors in the College of Engineering, but also the Juniors and most of the Sophomores; (3) the fact that once discontinued, the four-year course would be difficult to revive; (5) the fact that the times demand professional and technical training; (6) the hope that the increased effort put forth for this year to secure new students for next year's enrollment might result in a larger enrollment in the College of Engineering." (There was no item 4 in the board minutes.)

Graduation statistics from the 1930s will quantify the problems that President Kreinheder saw for maintaining the engineering college. The following table lists the average number of graduates per year from each division of the university in the periods 1931-1935 and 1936-1940.

	1931-35	1936-40
Arts and Sciences	51	48
Engineering	12	7
Law	7	10
Pharmacy	4	8

The college of engineering required a minimum of two professors for each of the three degree programs. Any reduction of staff was out of the question since each one was already teaching an average of nine different courses each year. The ratio of graduates to engineering faculty was nearing 1 during the last half of the decade. By comparison the ratio for arts and sciences was about 2 and for law it was 2.5. (The current ratio in the college of engineering is about 3.) Not only was the graduate-to-faculty ratio too low, the salary levels for the engineering faculty were above the average for the rest of the faculty. Yet, while engineering enrollment was low, engineering at Valparaiso was attracting its fair share of interest and student acceptance. As a fraction of the total student body, enrollment was well within national norms. Nevertheless, on average, slightly fewer than half of those who started the program graduated. This may have been due to the demands of the course or the poor preparation of the students, but certainly the economic hard times

Materials Testing Lab

took their toll. It is less likely that they left because they felt that the program was poor, since reminiscences of graduates from that era indicate that they felt they had been well prepared.

Despite the good will of the enrolled students, two other considerations leading to closure became prominent: one, the nature of the university; the other, its mission. The academic administration under President Kreinheder and Dean Kroencke had little previous experience with science-based professional programs. As financial difficulties continued, these administrators began to see the future of Valparaiso as a liberal arts college that they understood and could be comfortable with. Pharmacy was attracting very few Lutheran students, thus raising questions about its importance to a Lutheran university. Enrolling Lutheran students, however, did not seem to be a problem for engineering. The record indicates that the board kept the College of Engineering alive for several years. That it lasted until 1939 is due to the vision of board members who saw that it was important to educate Lutheran engineers.

Closing the College of Engineering

While the enrollment did not significantly improve at the start of the 1935-36 year, the economy did show signs of recovery and there was a modest increase in new students for the 1936-37 year. However, the untimely death of Dean Kroencke in September, 1936, evidently put the reorganization of academic programs on hold for a while. So, at the start of the 1937-38 year, the committee again took up the "engineering problem." The fate of the College of Pharmacy was also up for consideration. President Kreinheder reported to the board the committee's recommendation "that the University restrict its offerings in engineering to those courses ordinarily taught in the lower division of engineering schools." The board was not ready to act, however, and it referred the question of engineering and pharmacy back to the committee, with the understanding that the "resolution involved the carrying on of Pharmacy and Engineering for another year." In the summer of 1938, newly appointed Dean of the Faculty Walter G. Friedrich immediately began the steps necessary to move the committee's recommendation forward. When, at its October meeting, the board approved the closing of the College of Pharmacy in lieu of seeking re-accreditation of the college, Dean Friedrich immediately made arrangements with Purdue to accept the current freshman and sophomore pharmacy classes at the start of the 1939-40 year. The College of Pharmacy was maintained for that year so that the current junior class could graduate and be eligible for licensing exams.

How to effect the transition to a lower-division engineering program was a bit more complex, but by the January, 1939, board meeting, President Kreinheder was ready to make recommendations. Again citing the cost of maintaining a four-year program, he informed the board that Dean Friedrich had virtually completed arrangements with Dean Potter of Purdue to offer two types of cooperative plans with Purdue University. The first was labeled the "MIT Plan" and followed arrangements that MIT had developed with certain sister schools. The plan required that students complete three years of engineering and liberal studies at the sister school before entering MIT for the last two years of engineering. Students would earn a Bachelor of Arts degree from Valparaiso and a

Bachelor of Science degree from Purdue with this plan. The second was labeled the "Evansville Plan" after an arrangement that was already in place between Evansville College and Purdue University. In this plan students would complete the first two years of the Purdue curriculum at Valparaiso and only a Purdue degree would be earned. With the board's approval of these arrangements, the College of Engineering would revert to a department in the College of Arts and Sciences. President Kreinheder informed the board that "this department will be fully accredited by Purdue, our state technological school. In other words, for the first time in its history, every unit of Valparaiso will be accredited."

Electrical Lab

This claim, of course, was not strictly true since ECPD accredited only programs that awarded degrees. Therefore, Purdue would have to certify that the work taken at Valparaiso had met Purdue and ECPD standards. The new plan did give Valparaiso students a path to an accredited degree, reflecting the importance that Valparaiso placed on being able to tell prospective students that the university was fully accredited. President Kreinheder concluded his 1939 report to the board with these encouraging words, "By authorizing these steps, the Board of Directors will make it possible, for the first time, for our Lutheran young men to combine in one undergraduate curriculum sound training for Christian leadership in an accredited Lutheran institution and a thorough technological training in one of the greatest technological schools in the United States."

The board of directors approved the recommendations and the agreements with Purdue were completed. Dean Friedrich informed the board at a later meeting that year that the University of Michigan would also accept Valparaiso students on the same terms as Purdue. For those students in their third year when the changes were announced, the courses for the fourth year were offered during 1939-40. To mesh with Purdue's curriculum the new two-year curriculum was somewhat revised. There is no record of the difficulties faced by transferring sophomores whose course work was not consistent with curricula at other accredited engineering schools. The 11 graduates of 1940 were the last to receive VU degrees until 1951.

The Valparaiso University Bulletin formally announced the new arrangements for engineering education in the March, 1939, edition: "Valparaiso University has the honor to announce that it has concluded arrangements with Purdue University for two cooperative plans for engineering education which are similar to those recently inaugurated by Massachusetts Institute of Technology, Carnegie Institute of Technology, and other eminent technological schools. These plans make it possible for young men to combine in one curriculum a broad engineering education at a small university and an excellent advanced engineering training in one of the best technological schools in the world." The announcement made reference to the profession's desire for more liberal education in the engineering curriculum. It quoted W. E. Wickenden, now president of the Case School of Applied Science, "Young engineers in three cases out of four begin their careers in the realm of technical duties, but by the age of forty, three out of five are occupied with administrative duties." Also referenced in the announcement was a survey of 4000 recent engineering graduates taken by SPEE in which 60% indicated that they considered cultural courses indispensable for the modern engineer.

The two plans were labeled Plan I (Five-Year Plan) and Plan II (Four-Year Plan). Curricula were established leading to degrees in chemical, civil, electrical, and mechanical engineering at Purdue. The usual two years of mathematics through calculus, a year of chemistry, and a year of freshman composition were common to both plans in the first two years.

In Plan I, physics was taken in the third year instead of the second. In the freshman year, those taking Plan I replaced a shop laboratory and surveying with modern foreign language courses and a non-technical elective with a religion course. Those on the four-year plan were not required to take a second religion course since those credits would not be accepted by Purdue. The most significant change in the four-year plan was the replacement of three engineering courses with two courses in English literature and one in economics. This change achieved the emphasis on cultural content desired by the engineering profession, previously missing from the Valparaiso degrees. All but future chemical engineers took the descriptive geometry course, and only mechanical and electrical engineers took the second shop course. The chemical engineers took two additional chemistry courses. Those who elected the five-year plan added a second year of foreign language, two social science electives, a third religion course, two accounting courses and two other non-technical electives in addition to the technical courses required in the four-year plan.

Faculty and Students in the 30s

By the time the College of Engineering was closed, the faculty had been reduced to two. In the fall of 1940 only Dr. Moody, now acting head of the department, and Professor Moses Uban, B.S.M.E., constituted the engineering faculty. Donald D. Mallory, M.S.E.E; Herman Blickensderfer, B.S.C.E; Paul A. Cushman, Ph.D.; and Carl W. Lauritzen, M.S.E.E. also had faithfully served the University during difficult economic times that included two 10% wage reductions. Dean Moody and Professor Blickensderfer taught the mechanics and civil engineering courses. The mechanical engineering and shop courses were taught by Dr. Cushman and Professor Uban. Professors Mallory and Lauritzen taught the drawing and electrical engineering courses. Both Professors Cushman and Mallory left at the end of the 1938-1939 academic year and Professors Blickensderfer and Lauritzen left when the college was closed.

Several engineering graduates from this era of the College of Engineering developed ongoing relationships with Valparaiso University. Paul

Professor Uban and Students

Brandt, Class of 1933, served as a member of the Valparaiso University board of directors from 1951 to 1994, many of those years as chairman. He endowed the Brandt Professorship in Engineering and the Brandt Professorship in Marketing in the College of Business Administration. The Valparaiso community remembers his name in the Brandt Residence Hall. Robert C. Moellering, also from the Class of 1933, served on the board from 1936 to 1983 and also served as chairman. He is reputed to be the person who procured "Founders' Rock." Paul Fleck, a 1937 graduate, served for many years on the national advisory board and then on the board of directors from 1972 to 1983. Also serving first on the national advisory board and then as a member of the board of directors from 1968 to 1987 was William Tatman, Class of 1940. The family of Alfred Sieving, Class of 1937, endowed the Alfred W. Sieving Professorship in Engineering in his honor. He spent his entire engineering career at the Caterpillar Corporation where he was recognized as an outstanding heavy equipment designer.

Factors Leading to the Closure

The closure of the pharmacy and engineering colleges was a direct result of the general financial problems of the new Lutheran administration. With North Central Association accreditation achieved in 1929, the next order of business was to put the university on a firmer financial footing and make improvements to the physical plant and campus surroundings. Supporters and administration expended much effort in the 1930s on various fund raising drives and public relations efforts to raise awareness of Valparaiso among Lutheran Church-Missouri Synod pastors and laymen who had little understanding of church-related liberal and professional education. These efforts were neither total failures nor unqualified successes, and the administration increasingly had to focus on staying economically viable in the face of declining enrollment. Between 1931 and 1935 enrollment had dropped from 627 to 446; it remained in the upper 400 range for the rest of the decade.

As the decade of the 1930s began, the environs of the university buildings hardly looked like anyone's idea of a college campus. The most pressing physical plant needs were to improve the general appearance of the campus area and to construct a new gymnasium. After removing the old and outdated buildings from those acquired in 1925, administrators turned their attention to purchasing the remaining privately owned land and buildings which were mixed in among university holdings in the

Machine Shop

area of the Auditorium. This successful effort, along with the removal of Locust Street east of the Science building, created a more pleasing campus environment. Already in the early 1930s plans were formulated to raise money for the construction of a gym, but various difficulties, including disagreements with the architect, delayed the start. Finally, ground was broken for what is now Hilltop Gym in September, 1938.

As important as high costs and low enrollment were in closing the college and entering into cooperative arrangements with Purdue, the issue of accreditation may have been equally important. From the onset of Lutheran ownership, offering accredited programs was considered essential to the ultimate viability of the University. In an interview many years later, Dean Friedrich recalled how he had become convinced through an informal conversation with the executive of the pharmacy accreditation association that the association's objective was to eliminate small programs like Valparaiso's and that there was absolutely nothing that Valparaiso could do that would allow it to keep the accreditation that it currently held. While there is no record that a similar statement had been forthcoming from ECPD, it is most likely that the Valparaiso administration knew its chances for engineering accreditation were slim to non-existent. Well into the 1950s a significant minority of engineering educators believed that small, exclusively undergraduate engineering programs had no place in the national engineering education scheme.

Accrediting Engineering Programs Begins

The impetus for the founding of ECPD in 1932 had come from a recommendation in the final Wickenden Report for an organization that would establish standards for engineering education and conduct reviews of programs in terms of their quality and compliance. Initial on-site reviews were conducted by teams of educators in 1936 and 1937, with 102 schools having all or some of their programs accredited in this first round. Almost all of them were either state universities or well-established larger private schools. In Indiana only Purdue and Rose Polytechnic received initial ECPD accreditation. Apparently no program was "grandfathered" in. Since ECPD accredited degree programs rather than schools, some schools either did not submit all programs for review or did not gain initial acceptance for some of their programs. This was particularly true for chemical engineering programs.

A close reading of the Wickenden Report shows also an intention to define the mission of engineering colleges in the rapidly growing industrial economy of the 20th century. Central to this mission was the creation of new knowledge through academic research. For a number of years, smaller private colleges such as Ohio Northern, Bradley, Dayton, Tri-State, and the Milwaukee School of Engineering remained unaccredited. If schools had no graduate programs that supported research, the bar for accreditation was raised quite high. Even Northwestern University and the University of Notre Dame were not accepted on the first round.

A review of the Valparaiso curriculum of the 1930s shows that, even without the bias against small, wholly undergraduate programs, it would not have gained ECPD approval since it lacked a strong cultural component. While most engineering programs had been established in the context of undergraduate liberal arts colleges and not as stand-alone professional programs like law, medicine, and theology, over the years many programs had focused on specialized courses that had little classroom interaction, except for mathematics and science, with the rest of the undergraduate experience. The message was very clear in the Wickenden Report that experiences in the liberal arts were necessary if engineers were to rise to positions of influence in the economic and political life of the nation. Through accreditation by ECPD the profession meant to make the curriculum provide those experiences.

The 1938-1939 Valparaiso engineering curriculum is an example of how narrow many programs had become. Except for two freshman English courses, a Bible course, and an engineering-oriented economics course, the entire 144 credits were allocated to science, mathematics, and engineering. Certainly ECPD would not have recognized the Bible course and would most likely have classified the remaining three courses as skill courses rather than cultural courses. In light of what the engineering profession was requiring for accreditation, it is somewhat surprising that Valparaiso made no apparent effort to liberalize the engineering curriculum.

The 1940 "Aims and Scope of Engineering Curricula" Report

Having fostered the successful creation of ECPD, SPEE immediately took up the question of how to professionalize engineering even further. Under the guidance of Professor H. P. Hammond, in March, 1940, the Society issued a "Report of Committee on Aims and Scope of Engineering Curricula." The impetus for forming this committee came from the profession's strong interest in increasing the undergraduate curricula to five or six years. As part of such a plan, the committee expressed interest in requiring two years of study in schools of liberal arts before admission to the engineering school. Valparaiso's cooperative plan with Purdue, primarily a measure for solving pressing financial problems, was also clearly in line with the thinking of this portion of the engineering profession.

The report began by listing current problems:
1) "There is widespread insistence that the technological profession should be competent to evaluate the social problems with which they deal and to recognize the social forces which they create." 2) "There is a concerted effort toward a clearer definition of professional status and function coupled with higher qualifying standards and more adequate safeguards for both the practitioner and the public." 3) There is a "movement to make education beyond the secondary school more widely available and to postpone entry upon specialized study until a preliminary period of general study in college had been completed." 4) "There is difficulty in giving adequate attention to the rapid advances in science and technology within the confines of a four-year curriculum." 5) There is a need to find ways to increase the "thoroughness and breadth of instruction in fundamental matters and of stimulating among students initiative, resourcefulness, and originality."

The conclusions of the report were guided by the following basic assumption:

> It must be borne in mind, however, that the present engineering colleges constitute almost the sole agency for preparing young men for technological pursuits. For the common good, therefore, technological education must be kept widely available, its admission requirements should correspond to the present needs and interests of young men, and the terminal points should conform to the varied needs of industry and the public service as well as the standards of admission to the engineering profession. Until other types of institutions are established in sufficient numbers to assume a significant part of the burden, satisfaction of these needs must be the duty of the engineering college. In view of their broad function and their complex relationships, we consider it neither feasible nor socially desirable for the present group of engineering colleges to limit their aim to the preparation of young men for professional registration and practice.

The essential recommendation of the report was to maintain an integrated four-year undergraduate education suitable both for general technological work and for further professional study at the graduate level. The integrated curriculum should have both "scientific-technological" and "humanistic-social" studies. It should concentrate on fundamentals in the undergraduate curriculum and shift the more advanced engineering work to the post-baccalaureate period: "Its roots should extend more deeply into the social sciences and humanities as well as into the physical sciences in order to sustain a rounded educational growth which will continue into professional life." There was also concern that if the engineering colleges limited themselves to admitting their students at the junior-senior level, they would lose control of the quality of the basic engineering, mathematics, and science courses. By favoring an integrated undergraduate program rather than one divided into separate stages, the report validated Valparaiso's integrated program with Purdue but also left the door open for Valparaiso to resume its four-year program in the future when conditions improved.

SIX

A Venture of Faith: 1940-1951

On October 6, 1940, Otto Paul Kretzmann was inaugurated as president of Valparaiso University, its third under the Lutheran ownership. He came to Valparaiso from the position of executive secretary of the Walther League, a national organization for young adult and high-school-age Missouri Synod Lutherans. A 39 year old bachelor, he had been with the Walther League for 6 years, following 10 years as a professor at Concordia Seminary in Springfield, Illinois. While he had no real experience in college administration, he brought to Valparaiso his prominence among leading, forward-looking Lutheran intellectuals and a solid record in bringing the Walther League to a position of importance in the lives of the young people of the Church. For the next 28 years O.P., as he was known to almost everyone, inspired a generation of students, faculty, and supporters to transform a struggling small college into a true university and a leader in Lutheran higher education.

The arrival of President Kretzmann coincided with the elimination of the full four-year engineering programs. As young men went off to war, enrollment in the pre-engineering program declined. To sustain the vision of engineering education at Valpo and to boost enrollment in the engineering courses, liberal arts students were encouraged to enroll in basic engineering courses for elective credit. With the conclusion of the war in 1945, enrollment in the cooperative program with Purdue was sufficient to encourage the administration to consider reinstituting the College of Engineering and its three degree programs. What happened then is a defining event in the history of Valparaiso University now known as the "Venture of Faith."

The Challenges of World War II

In his inaugural address, Kretzmann began by referring to the war which had already been raging for a year in Europe, and in Asia since 1937: "By this time even the most optimistic observer of the course of human events knows that the world has come to an hour of crisis in the life of man which threatens to destroy all the values of Western civilization as we have known it since the Church emerged from the catacombs. We have come now to the winter of the modern world, and there are few signs of spring." America had already begun mobilizing for war. A few weeks earlier, in September, 1940, Congress had passed the Selective Service Act, subjecting all men between 21 and 30 to selection by lottery for one year's service in the army. Industry geared up to produce war materials for export to England, helping the country to shake off the effects of the economic depression. When England ran out of money to pay, in March, 1941, Congress passed a Lend-Lease Act which continued export of war material without payment. America entered the war in both Asia and Europe in December, 1941, and the draft was extended to all men 18-45 with no limit on length of service. In its wake, the collapse of male enrollment that had nearly bankrupted the university in 1917 was about to happen again.

Under the leadership of President Kretzmann, the enrollment problem was vigorously attacked. It was probably a combination of better economic times, the personal magnetism of President Kretzmann among the youth of the Church, and the addition of a second staff member responsible for recruiting new students that resulted in a 20% increase in enrollment for the 1941-42 year. Another 10% increase the following year was very encouraging, particularly since most colleges were suffering enrollment declines due to the war. That decline hit Valparaiso in 1943, as more young men and women went off to war or to work in the war industries. However, the increases of the two previous years were enough to encourage the administration to believe that when the war ended it could expect a student population of as many as 900 students.

One effect of the war was that the student body, historically mostly male, had become primarily female. Moreover, this increase in female students was seen as an opportunity to permanently increase enrollment. To achieve this objective the university needed to make its programs and facilities more attractive to women. In 1943 social work, home economics, and physical education were added, and the Lutheran

Deaconess Association located its training program at Valparaiso. Also in 1943, architect Edward Jannson was engaged to plan a new women's residence hall. The story is told that, considering where to build this dormitory, he looked to the east of the new gymnasium and suggested to the board members with him that the university should own that land. The board members took him up on his suggestion and authorized Albert Scribner, the business manager of the university, to obtain options to buy the various tracts in the area east of McIntyre Court all the way to Sturdy Road and south to US 30. Six board members formed a corporation and purchased the land for $42,792 in April, 1944. In June, they sold the land to the university for $35,095, taking promissory notes instead of cash as payment.

By June, 1944, the prosecution of the war had turned in the Allies' favor, and victory was all but certain. The Russians had gained control on the eastern front and American and British forces had successfully gained a foothold in France. In the Pacific, American forces were slowly advancing, one island at a time. Congress felt sure enough about the outcome to pass the Servicemen's Readjustment Act, better known as the GI Bill of Rights, which provided tuition and expenses for college or vocational training to all military veterans. The University saw this legislation as another opportunity to increase enrollment. Using lists supplied by the Armed Forces Commission of the Missouri Synod, it sent information to more than 70,000 Lutheran service-men about to be released from armed service, and hoped that better days were ahead for Valparaiso University.

To accommodate the expected influx of students, the board and administration worked toward creating more student housing and approved the plan to build the Guild and Memorial women's residence

Donald D. Mallory

Donald Mallory was the first mechanical engineering graduate from Valparaiso, earning his degree in 1928. A native of Cuyahoga Falls, Ohio, he joined the faculty in 1929, teaching drawing and electrical engineering courses. In 1936, while teaching at Valparaiso, he earned an M.S.E.E. from the University of Michigan by attending there during summer sessions. When the college closed

halls as soon as materials and labor would be available. The vision and faith of the board to make such bold plans for the future of Valparaiso University at a time when the enrollment had declined to a mere 300 students is admirable. For, not only housing, but additional classrooms and laboratories were needed if Valparaiso were to prosper in the post-war years.

THE DEPARTMENT OF ENGINEERING DURING THE WAR

The start of the Kretzmann administration coincided with the official end of the College of Engineering as a four-year degree granting program and its reorganization as a department in the College of Arts and Sciences. By the fall of 1940, the faculty had been reduced to two: Dean, now Professor, Moody and Moses Uban. Enrollment records from this period are not broken down by major so we can not determine the number of students choosing the cooperative arrangement with Purdue, but three pieces of evidence indicate that the enrollment was encouraging. First, at the October, 1941, board meeting, President Kretzmann reported increased enrollment in the department of engineering. Second, he also reported that Donald Mallory, who had left for the University of Wyoming in 1939, had accepted appointment as chairman of the department of engineering at a wage of $3,000. (This salary equaled that of Dean Friedrich and was higher than that of any other member of the faculty.) Third, a group picture in *The Beacon* (the yearbook newly renamed from *The Uhlan*, which had German militaristic connotations) showed 31 engineers posed with their tools of the trade: slide rules, transits, drawing instruments, and a model bridge truss. Among the students was freshman Fred Kruger, a future dean of the

> he took a teaching position at the University of Wyoming in 1939, but returned to Valparaiso as head of the department of engineering in the fall of 1941, replacing Dr. Moody. In March, 1943, he was given a leave to join a war research project at MIT. His leave was continued to the end of the 1944-1945 year as Professor and Head and a further year as Professor but he never returned to Valparaiso. An early 1950s photograph of him in the university archive carries the notation that he was Chief Engineer of the American Safety Razor Company of Cedar Knolls, New Jersey.

college. Professor Mallory's re-appointment showed the administration's optimism about both current demand and the future of the program.

The United States entered the war in December, 1941. President Kretzmann reported to the board in January, 1942, "Despite the alarming decrease in enrollment at other schools and colleges, there has been little change at Valpo." This claim, however, was short-lived. Starting in 1942, the government requested that all colleges operate year-round as part of the war effort. Valparaiso complied. By the fall semester of 1943, enrollment had declined from a record high of 552 in 1942 to about 100 men and 200 women. Students graduated "early" and fewer students enrolled. No data is available for engineering enrollment but one can assume that it also dropped proportionately. Already in 1941, to improve enrollment in engineering courses, liberal arts students were allowed to use 6 credits of engineering courses for their degrees. The president reported that "liberal arts students have flocked to these courses."

During the war younger professors were given leaves to participate in military service. In April, 1943, Donald Mallory was given a leave to participate in the war effort by being involved in a government research and development project in electronics (probably radar development) at MIT. He was replaced by Harold Mummert, a 1930 mechanical engineering graduate of Purdue who had also attended Valparaiso. While on leave, Professor Mallory continued to be listed as head of the department of engineering until 1946 when Moses Uban was named acting head. Mallory never returned to teach at Valparaiso. In April of 1944, President Kretzmann reported to the board that the university had signed a contract for engineering professors Uban and Mummert, physics professor Ancil Thomas, and chemistry professor Walter Thrun to do research for Alten's Foundry and Machine Works of Ohio, whose owner was a supporter of the University. Since this was a contract with the university, it is reasonable to assume that the arrangement was made to offset the salaries of these professors who, by 1944, had very few students to teach. The arrangement continued for at least five years. Their initial project was to determine the reasons for the unexpected failures of steel molds that the foundry was producing for the Ball Brothers Glass Company.

The facilities for engineering instruction were located in the Engineering Building at the southwest corner of College and Union Streets. Constructed in 1880 as the Commerce Building, it became the Engineering Building in 1928. With the prospect of an influx of engineering students at the end of the war, the administration ordered an in-house survey of its condition in 1944. The building was found to be structurally unsafe and unfit for long-term instructional purposes. If the leadership of the university wanted seriously to consider eliminating the engineering program, this report would have given it the opportunity. However, the board record is silent about any such discussions.

With the surrender of Japan on August 15, 1945, World War II officially ended. Enrollment in September soared to 742 from about 300 just two years earlier. Of these 742, 78 were registered for the VU-Purdue cooperative engineering course. This show of interest required a serious re-assessment of the condition and use of the Engineering Building. In October, 1945, the board considered the 1944 report, allocated $1800 for a new roof, and ordered a professional evaluation of the building. In May, 1946, the university received a report from J. M. McConnell, a structural engineer from Chicago, who concluded, "This building is not suitable for an Engineering Building, where loads are fairly heavy and moving machinery is used. This building has a very limited life and we could not recommend that much money be expended upon repairs." Further he stated, "This building should be used only for very light loads and, if used at all, the following repairs should be made: The waterproofing of all exterior surfaces of walls; strengthening of the roof girders; and if the west wing, third floor, is used, the girders supporting this floor should be strengthened. The above alterations will not be very expensive and will extend the life of the building." Among his additional observations were these: "The brick walls of this building are constructed of salmon hand made brick laid up in lime mortar; the brick being covered on the exterior with a stucco finish. The mortar joints are disintegrating due to the absorption of moisture; these soft bricks being very absorbent," and "The first floor joists for a major portion of the building are in contact with the earth and cannot be in a very good condition."

Preparing for an Expected Influx of Engineering Students

At the conclusion of the war, the federal government established a program of distributing surplus material to colleges to help them meet the many demands of the service men and women who were going to enroll under the GI Bill. Within two years, the university had acquired one large and two small frame dormitory buildings, a number of house trailers for married veterans, a complex of frame classroom and laboratory buildings, a cafeteria, and set of buildings to house its physical plant services. During the fall term of 1945, Professor Uban and chemistry professor Raymond Larson were delegated to search for useful engineering and scientific equipment from the available war surplus. President Kretzmann reported to the board in January, 1946, "Professors Uban and Larson spent much of their time during the last three months locating surplus government equipment in industrial plants. Prof. Uban reports that we have $15,000 worth of useable equipment designated to the university." Professor Uban requested an additional $5000 to purchase this equipment. What to do with it after it arrived was going to be a problem. The May, 1946, report on the condition of the Engineering Building made it clear that any heavy machine tool equipment for the course "Shop Laboratory: Machine Tool Work" could not be installed there.

The administration was anticipating that several hundred engineering students would enroll for the fall semester of 1946 (the actual number turned out to be 245). At the same time that it was considering the needed repairs for the Engineering Building, the board selected the J. W. Snyder Company of Chicago to build Guild and Memorial Halls. The cornerstone for this most financially ambitious project of the Lutheran administration was laid in September, 1946. Despite the major fundraising and construction commitment to build Guild and Memorial Halls, the board allocated $15,000 to clean up and repair the Engineering Building and authorized a new building for the shop equipment. Late in that summer, the Smith-Nuppnau Company of Valparaiso was contracted to construct a 6600 square foot concrete block building, to be known as the Engineering Annex, directly south of the Engineering Building on College Street for an estimated cost of $25,000. Its actual cost by the time it was completed and opened for use in February, 1947, was closer to $39,000. When it was completed in October, 1947, a total of $35,000 was spent on repairs to the Engineering Building, another cost overrun. The Engineering Annex was later renamed Moody Laboratory in honor of Dean Howard Moody; presently it is the home of the Hilltop Neighborhood Child Care Center.

Engineering Annex

Planning for the Return of the Four-year Program

With 245 engineering students enrolled for the 1946-1947 year, the board and administration began to think seriously about re-instituting a four-year program. Professor Carl A. Muhlenbruch of Carnegie Institute of Technology was employed as a consultant to evaluate the viability of such a move, and President Kretzmann presented his conclusions to the board at its January, 1947, meeting. In essence Professor Muhlenbruch's opinion was that degree programs in civil, electrical, and mechanical engineering were within the realm of possibility. He found that the existing laboratory equipment for civil and electrical engineering was either adequate or could be made so with minimal investment but that equipment for the advanced mechanical engineering courses was inadequate. Citing difficulties with housing the laboratory apparatus, securing classroom space, and adding faculty, he proposed a phased process of adding one program each year starting with civil, then electrical, and finally mechanical engineering. The board appointed an ad-hoc committee of board members to meet with Muhlenbruch, Uban, and business manager Scribner in Chicago in early March to consider the proposal. In his March report to the board, President Kretzmann concluded that the only real impediment to the plan was the "question of finances." A decision was put off until the August board meeting. At that time, once again demonstrating its commitment to an engineering program, the board resolved to re-establish the four-year engineering programs at a time that finances could be secured.

Underscoring the board's optimism, the following article appeared in the December, 1947, edition of the *Valparaiso University Bulletin*, a general publication sent to supporters of the University:

> Due to the decision of the Board of Directors, it may soon not be necessary for many of the 300 engineering students to transfer at the end of two or three years to other schools to complete the more technical part of their training. Surveys made by visiting engineers and the Valparaiso administration, careful study of facilities, equipment, staff and course offerings indicate that before long it will be possible to restore the four-year courses in civil and electrical engineering.
>
> The cooperative plans conducted with Purdue University have successfully fulfilled their purpose: that of enabling prospective engineers to attend the Lutheran University for at least part of their training while Valparaiso groomed and overhauled its own engineering program. Now, however, the greatly increased student demands coupled with the admirable job of collecting machinery directed by Prof. M. W. Uban, acting head of the department, make it advisable to restore the full four years as soon as possible. How soon? That, the Board said, depends upon when the necessary funds are available for the final steps. In the meantime, several hundred thousand dollars worth of machinery, acquired at slight cost from war surplus, is rapidly

being put to use in the new Engineering Annex. Extensive renovation is taking place in the old building, also, in preparation for the four-year program.

Even as planning was going forward, some unanswered questions still remained. President Kretzmann, in his report to the board in January, 1948, indicated that he had "asked President D. B. Prentice of Rose Polytechnic Institute to make a thorough survey of our facilities. President Prentice will be on our campus some time during the next month and I hope that the results of his examination will enable us to present some definite figures in the April meeting of the board." He also noted, "the demand for the additional two years is growing steadily more insistent." The Report of the President prepared for the May 8, 1948, board meeting summarized the findings of President Prentice. He agreed that the University could support programs in civil, electrical, and mechanical engineering. He was favorably impressed with the quality of instruction and the available laboratory equipment. But he felt "very keenly, that an additional building would be a primary requirement." President Prentice had suggested that a building similar to one recently constructed at the University of Delaware would fit Valparaiso's requirement very well, and business manager Scribner was delegated to find out more about this building.

Some time after having received the report from President Prentice, President Kretzmann conducted a meeting with the entire engineering student body. He found that their enthusiasm for reinstituting the four-year program was "clearly evident" and heard their offers to help make it happen. As a result of this meeting, another meeting of engineering students was held on April 21, 1948. In a memorandum to President Kretzmann in early May, Professor George Reuss summarized the outcome of the meeting and the proposals made by the student leaders. He reported that the students volunteered to conduct a financial campaign to raise a portion of the funds required for the building. They realized that their campaign would provide only a small portion of the required capital, but they felt that their efforts would encourage more active support from friends of the university and make the work of the public relations department less difficult. They also asked, "Can we, the students, help build the new engineering building?" Professor Reuss observed that several students were most enthusiastic and "surprisingly realistic" in their approach to the problem. The plan they suggested required that construction of three laboratory sections of the building be completed at the earliest possible date for use in the fall term of 1949. Classrooms for the engineering building would then need to be completed as soon as possible. He felt that the talent available in this class was better than average and estimated that a group of 20-25 students working over the summer would be very productive and economical. He said that the students would like to be paid 50 cents per hour plus room and board, but he was not sure how much of the total labor cost this would save. The students had also obtained the assistance of Mr. Milan Morgan, a registered engineer and part-time instructor in surveying, to help plan the building. Professor Reuss concluded his memorandum as follows: "The answer to the students' question is not easily given. Students are realistic and several are helpful. With approval of the Board of Directors, these same students could in four weeks time and with proper guidance make more specific suggestions and have answers for more specific questions which will arise in the minds of the Board of Directors."

Engineering Laboratory with Heine Hall in the background

In his report to the board, President Kretzmann concluded his analysis of the situation as follows:

> It is evident from all these considerations that our entire problem resolves itself into a financial one. If a way can be found to gather the necessary support for this particular project it would be entirely feasible. On the other hand, the members of the Board will be deeply aware of the implications of any new project under our present financial circumstances. I therefore recommend:
>
> A. That the Board re-affirm its resolution of last October to introduce the four years of engineering at the earliest possible moment.
>
> B. That the Buildings and Grounds Committee and the Administration of the University be instructed to study the problem of the costs and to present a detailed analysis at the next meeting of the Board. The study should include the possibility of using student labor in the construction of the laboratories.

But the board did not follow this recommendation. Student leaders Glenn Colley and Blair Hawkins were invited to make a presentation at the meeting of the plans the students had developed. Glenn Colley, in his prepared remarks at the 50th class-reunion in 2001 remembered the story this way:

> Fifty-three years ago – 'Wow!'. What experiences we had as students of Valpo in initiating, planning and building the Engineering Laboratory. In February of 1948, a meeting was held in the Chapel Auditorium, with President O.P. Kretzmann addressing the group. The question was raised, 'Why can't the University reinstall a four-year program, and a College of Engineering?' President Kretzmann advised us that the University did not have the resources to expand from a department to a full college, with a need for additional faculty, lab equipment, and housing for the lab. The students then said 'If we build the lab building, will the University staff and equip it?' The President then asked for show of hands as to the real interest of the group. This was unanimous, so he gave us a 'yes' answer.

Colley recalled how he and Blair Hawkins, at the suggestion of President Kretzmann, had visited individual board members before the meeting to explain their plans and ask for their support. Board treasurer John Sauerman told them that, while he supported their plans, "he would bet his shirt that they would not get the permission of the labor unions for students to construct the building." As the time for the board meeting approached, the students had won approval from all union trades except the local carpenters union. Colley and Hawkins traveled to Indianapolis where the International Carpenters Union was meeting and persuaded the international president to support their plan. The president even volunteered to be with them when they presented their proposals to the board. The local carpenters union gave its approval the day before the board meeting. As the student committee presented its plans at the board meeting, the fact that the president of the International Carpenters Union was waiting in the hall in case there were questions made it very difficult for the board to reject or postpone the building project. Winning union approval so impressed the board that it included the complete text of the authorizing letter from the Porter County Trades Council in the meeting minutes. In his remarks at the reunion, Colley recalled that "it had been prearranged that if we got approval the bells would ring around the campus. What a beautiful sound that was! And the Venture of Faith was underway."

THE VENTURE OF FAITH BEGINS

Clearly the students' enthusiasm, planning, and attention to detail impressed the board members. Instead of delaying final consideration to a later board meeting as President Kretzmann had recommended in his report, they approved the project with this resolution:
1. That we encourage the student committee in the proposed project with the understanding that they carry out their part in its execution as presented in this meeting.
2. That the president of the university be instructed to appoint a committee to work with the students both in the execution of this resolution and the raising of the necessary funds.
3. That the department of public relations be directed to handle all the matter of publicity relative to the entire project.

A management team for the project was appointed immediately. It consisted of Milan Morgan as engineer and chief executive; Peter Baier, who had just completed a similar assignment in the construction of Guild and Memorial Halls, as full-time construction superintendent; registrar and business manager A. F. Scribner; assistant business manager Gale Morgan; and faculty members Kruger, who had joined the faculty that year, Uban, and Reuss. Representing the students were Glen Colley, Erwin Michalk, and Blair Hawkins. On June 8, 1948, the buildings and grounds committee of the board met with this team to approve the site selection in the "Dust Bowl" north of the corner of Linwood and Mound and to finalize construction details. The cornerstone was laid on July 24, 1948, in conjunction with the July board meeting. In late October, 66 students (10 in fund-raising and 56 in construction) were recognized as having made significant contributions to the construction of the building at a banquet hosted by Leonard Heine, an enthusiastic friend of Valparaiso from Omaha, Nebraska. By November Peter Baier reported that the building was enclosed and that the west section would be ready in January, 1949. The rest would be ready for the start of school by the following September.

Engineering Laboratory from the North

As it seems with all construction projects, the final cost was more than originally anticipated. The minutes of the June 8, 1948, meeting indicate that all believed the cost would be between $100,000 and $110,000 exclusive of equipment. The final accounting in December, 1949, listed $133,000 for construction charges of a 17,800 square foot building, or about $7.50 per square foot. An additional $6000 was spent on equipment. By way of comparison, the cost of the Engineering Annex constructed two years earlier was about $6.00 per square foot and Kroencke Hall, built three years later, cost about $13.30 per square foot. It would appear that student labor saved some cost, but a direct comparison is not easy for several reasons. There was significant inflation in the price of materials and labor in the years after the war; for example, the Consumer Price Index rose 22% between 1946 and 1949. The Engineering Laboratory required significantly more material for its interior spaces than did the Engineering Annex, and Kroencke Hall had considerably more volume and a more complicated roof structure than either of the other two buildings. Incorrect roof construction on the Engineering Laboratory required a $0.50 per square foot roof rebuild almost immediately. All this suggests some cost savings, but the real value of the student initiative lay not in the construction cost but in the publicity that the student initiative generated for Valparaiso University and in the $72,000 that was realized by the student-led fund raising campaign.

The College of Engineering is Re-established

At its December, 1948, meeting, the board officially re-established the department of engineering as the College of Engineering. The first order of business was to appoint a dean to organize and staff the college. On January 23, 1949, Herman C. Hesse, Professor of Mechanical Engineering at the Illinois Institute of Technology accepted the appointment. While he completed his assignment at IIT, he made regular trips to Valparaiso to help plan the introduction of the program and find faculty to staff it. He officially began his service in September, 1949, as the first junior class began its work.

Dean Hesse immediately took up the problem of finding classrooms for the new college. Consultant J. M. McConnell had found that the Engineering Building at College and Union Streets was structurally deficient and had recommended only very low-loading activities on the second and third floors. He had also recommended repairs that were at best only temporary. To meet some of the immediate needs, two spaces in the new Engineering Laboratory were temporarily converted into classrooms. With the exception of a drafting room on the first floor of the south wing and the wood shop on the second floor, use of the Engineering Building for instruction was ended. At the November, 1949, board meeting, Dean Hesse presented a plan for the engineering classrooms as phase two of the engineering building project. This plan was a T-shaped building of construction similar to that of the Engineering Laboratory with six general classrooms and three offices totaling 6144 square feet at the top of the T and three drafting rooms totaling 3360 square feet on the upright of the T. The building and grounds committee asked for authorization to present detailed plans at the next board meeting. However, no immediate action was taken. The need was evident, but the money was not.

Under construction with the "historic" sign

In the meantime, a small construction project did take place. Having received a gift of $5,000 from Leonard Heine, in the summer of 1950 Professor Kruger and students Bill Aszman and Otto Woike constructed a small frame house-type building as a laboratory for heating, ventilating, and air conditioning. Built on the top of the hill to the west of the Engineering Laboratory, this building contained a main room used for small classes and a library, two small rooms that became faculty offices, and a room containing the HVAC equipment. This building, officially called Heine Hall, was destroyed by an arsonist who also burned the Medical Building (Heimlich Hall) and several other buildings in the city of Valparaiso.

Kroencke Hall

In a series of decisions related to the pressures for more classrooms brought on by increased enrollment and the desire to add a program in elementary education, the building for engineering classrooms proposed by Dean Hesse as phase two of the plan for the College of Engineering became a building to meet broader needs. The outbreak of the Korean War in June, 1950, heightened the concern that the university would again start losing male enrollment as it had during World War II. Once again thinking about making the university more attractive to women students, the administration concluded that the absence of an elementary education program had resulted in the loss of significant numbers of new students. This program had been dropped in 1933, partly out of concern that the university would be seen as competing with the Missouri Synod's Concordia Teachers Colleges. Now though, administrators resolved to begin elementary education as early as possible, preferably in September, 1951. However, a survey of spaces that could house such a program indicated that no space could be allocated to the program. In addition to the classroom needs previously reported for the new engineering courses, this survey also highlighted the acute needs of the department of business and economics and the School of Law in the Arts-Law (DeMotte) building, adequate spaces for studios in art, and the inappropriate use of the basement of Lembke Hall for workshops for the department of speech and drama.

These concerns prompted the suggestion at the November, 1950, board meeting that a new building to meet these needs should be built in the remaining space between the new Engineering Laboratory and the Gymnasium. To finance this building, estimated to cost between $150,000 and $200,000, the university would request that the Lutheran Layman's League (LLL) reallocate the money it had already raised for the proposed administration building. The board pledged to replace this money when the full $500,000 had been raised by the LLL. Since there was some overlap between the boards of the university and the LLL, details were worked out by January, 1951, and rough construction plans and estimates made by the Smith-Nuppnau Company were presented to the board. The estimated cost for construction was $145,000. Desiring to have the building complete by the start of the fall semester, the board entered into a "cost plus fee" contract for construction, in spite of the warning by board member Robert Moellering, who owned his own construction company, that the cost could ultimately rise to $200,000. (It turned out that he was only a few thousand too high.) Dean Hesse was given the responsibility of representing the university in working with the contractor to design and construct the building. Not surprisingly, the building turned out to look very much like the one he had proposed a year earlier, with the drafting rooms replaced by an auditorium and stage. Since it was a "fast-track" project, detailed design continued after construction began. Studios for art were moved from Science (Baldwin Hall) to the new building and the vacated space was assigned to the new elementary education program. The speech and drama department moved its materials from the basement of Lembke Hall. While the new building solved the need for engineering classrooms, it did not solve the entire need for engineering drafting rooms. While one drafting room used for upper-division design courses was located in the new building, the large general drafting room remained in the Engineering Building. Not liking the working name of Engineering and Dramatic Arts Building, the executive committee of the board named it the Dean F. W. Kroencke Memorial Building.

The Venture of Faith Film

No history of the College of Engineering would be complete without the story of the movie that gives this chapter its name: "Venture of Faith." One of the major projects of the Lutheran Layman's League, in addition to its production of the syndicated radio program "The Lutheran Hour," was the production of movies tailored for audiences of Lutheran church groups. Having produced a successful film about the dangers of atheistic communism, its leadership felt that a film promoting the value of Christian higher education would be of interest, especially since the LLL was at that time also raising money for the LLL Memorial Building at Valparaiso. In late 1949 producer T. G. Eggers proposed a film about the construction of the Engineering Laboratory. In April, 1950, the board gave its support to the project and readily agreed to the use of the campus as needed. Filming was carried out in the spring of 1951, using Hollywood actors in the major roles and professional production crews. By no stretch of the imagination a documentary, it was, as the introduction stated, "based upon truth. It is not an attempt to recreate the precise facts of this story." Various campus locations were used for scenes and a number of faculty and administrators had bit parts unrelated to their campus positions. Dean Hesse, however, did play the part of the engineering dean and President Kretzmann played himself. Construction scenes were filmed during the actual construction of

Moses Walter Uban

Moses Uban was born on April 30, 1890, on a farm near Lake Ariel, Pennsylvania, a community east of Scranton. As for many boys on farms in that era, a high school education meant leaving home to board in a community that had a school. Also like many young people at that time, he came to Valparaiso to complete his last two years of high school in 1907. He stayed on at Valparaiso and began university studies, majoring in education. When his father became ill in 1913, he returned home. At his father's death a brother took over the family farm and he and another brother went east to Bridgeport, Connecticut, where they learned the tool-making trade at the Bullard Machine Tool Co. He later worked at both the Remington Arms Company and Singer Sewing Machine Company. With the outbreak of the war, he enlisted in the Army and was assigned to the Army Air Corps, but the war ended as he was being readied to embark to France.

Kroencke Hall. Winner of a Freedom Foundation Award, the film is now firmly part of the lore of the College of Engineering and is often shown as part of college social events.

Building a Faculty and a Curriculum

The engineering faculty at the start of the 1945-1946 year consisted of M. W. Uban (Acting Head), Howard Moody, and Harold Mummert. At the end of the school year, Professor Mummert resigned; he was replaced by George Reuss, an electrical engineering graduate of the University of Virginia. At the start of the 1947-48 year, Fred W. Kruger and at least four part-time instructors joined them to teach the 280 students now enrolled in engineering. The 1948-49 year began with 213 students, new full-time instructors Lewis Kiser and Robert Meyer, and four part-time instructors. In March, 1949, Professor Moody died after a brief illness. Joining Dean Hesse at the start of the 1949-50 academic year were Lewis Unnewehr, who replaced George Reuss, and Charles Peller, who replaced Dr. Moody. Five part-time instructors completed the roster. The following year the faculty for the four-year programs was completed with the appointment of Kenneth Mortimer and seven part-time instructors.

Of necessity, the curriculum was essentially Purdue's for those who had been freshmen in 1947 and 1948 and who were now going to complete their degree at Valparaiso. A Valparaiso curriculum was announced for

> He returned to Valparaiso and earned a Bachelor of Arts from the education department in 1922 and then assumed the position of assistant professor of English. He met his wife Evelyn when she was a paper grader for his English courses. During his student days he was a member of the Alpha Epsilon fraternity. In his last year as a degree student he was also an instructor in machine shop. In the immediate post-WWI the university was operating a federal government program to teach various trades to shell-shocked veterans of the war. The administration became aware that the teacher of the machine-shop trades was a spiritualist who was holding séances in his classes, which was not a good thing to be doing with veterans whose mental state was fragile. Since these courses were a reliable source of university income at a time when the general financial condition of Valparaiso was becoming dire, Uban was asked to take over the instruction of these courses. Thus was born the engineering career of Professor Uban.
>
> *Continued next page*

freshmen of 1949 by Professor Uban in December, 1948. Since no dean had yet been appointed, the administration asked Dean David Arm of the University of Delaware to review the proposed plan. He found it adequate with some minor revisions. The new curricula required 154 credits for CE, 153 for ME and 152 for EE. The first two years were common for all three programs except for one course in the fourth semester. Significant deletions for all majors were Surveying and Foundry & Pattern Making. Added for all programs were two one-credit freshman orientation courses and a shop course in manufacturing processes. Civil engineers were required to take a six-week summer surveying camp. All three programs had 101 credits in common; 29 in engineering and 72 in science, math, physical education, religion, English, public speaking, economics, contracts and specifications, and non-technical electives. The common engineering courses were statics, dynamics, and fluid mechanics, strength of materials, materials testing lab, and experimental stress analysis. Civil and mechanical engineers took two special electrical engineering courses and the civil and electrical engineers had a special thermodynamics course.

Extracurricular Traditions

After several weeks in which mysterious "Watch for TED" posters had everyone on the campus guessing, the freshman class of 1949 revealed

> By 1926 his title was instructor in engineering and machine shop and in 1930 he was instructor in engineering. During these years he began his own formal engineering education and earned the B.S.M.E. in 1932 from Valparaiso. When the engineering program was reduced to a two-year pre-engineering course he and Dean Moody became the entire engineering faculty. At the start of the 1941 academic year, he was given leave to become the coordinator of National Defense Training for the Calumet area. He returned to full time teaching in 1942. During the lean years of the war he also taught at the local high school and worked for Urschel Laboratories during the summer. From 1946 to 1949 he served as acting head of the department of engineering. He reached the mandatory retirement age of 70 in 1960. He died on January 26, 1963. From 1952 to 1958, his son Earl, a graduate of Valparaiso and Purdue in the 3-2 program, also taught in the College of Engineering. Professor Moses Uban was one of only two faculty members whose teaching careers spanned both the Brown-Kinsey and Lutheran eras.

that TED stood for The Engineers Day and that the Class of 1953 was inaugurating an annual Saturday afternoon of games and entertainment for all engineers on May 6, 1950. TED had been an annual banquet sponsored by the Engineering Society, first held on May 2, 1930. There is no record of when the first TED expired but Wilber "Tex" Gray is reputed to be the student who led its resurrection. As the longest running tradition of the College of Engineering, TED has taken several different forms, at present having evolved into an evening of food and fun held in February during National Engineers Week.

The Engineering Supply store was a non-profit enterprise initiated by the Engineering Society in 1948 or 1949 to provide students with quality drafting instruments and slide rules at prices below retail. It also sold other specialized items that did not compete with the University Book Store. A room for stock and sales was provided by the college. Prices were marked up enough to pay a reasonable salary to student managers and to produce a surplus that could provide funds for Engineering Society activities. For many years this surplus covered the major cost of the annual TED Banquet. By the 1990s computers had replaced slide rules, calculators, and paper-and-pencil drafting and the available mark-up on the miscellaneous supplies was not sufficient to pay for the time of the student manager. The supply store ceased operation in 1995, but over the years it had supplied valuable business experience for scores of engineering students.

The tradition of an "Engineering Train" pulled by freshmen in the annual homecoming parade began in the late 1940s. Each new class was expected to construct a freight car to add to the train. The length of the train did not grow as much as might be expected since often the freshmen spent their effort on repairing older cars. In later years a motorized engine was added. The tradition continued until the Engineering Building was razed and there was no place left to store the train.

SEVEN

FROM THE ENGINEERING LABORATORY TO GELLERSEN CENTER: 1951-1968

With the four-year program re-established and the move to the new laboratory building completed, the College of Engineering turned to achieving ECPD accreditation and solutions for the rest of its facilities problems. Accreditation was finally achieved in 1958 after an unsuccessful first attempt in 1955. Constructing Graland Hall provided adequate drafting rooms and made it possible to abandon the several-times-condemned Engineering Building.

Curriculum developments during the 1950s and 60s were influenced by both external and internal conditions. Engineering education leaders were chagrined by the fact that scientists and not engineers had made the significant contributions to the major technical advances of World War II. They commissioned another curriculum study, the outcome of which called for an increase in basic science and engineering science courses and the removal of outdated engineering practice subjects. These changes would better support the national defense needs during the developing Cold War. At Valparaiso the failed accreditation attempt in 1955 led to a complete reorganization of the physics faculty and curriculum. Physics instruction improved but high failure rates for engineering students caused friction between the college of engineering and the physics department, a situation which led to basic physics being taught by engineering faculty rather than physics faculty in 1964.

During the 1950s and 60s college enrollments continued to increase, causing severe shortages of housing and instructional facilities. In response to national defense needs during the Cold War, the federal government instituted programs to aid colleges in constructing and improving instructional facilities for science, mathematics, engineering, and modern foreign languages. Even though the engineering facilities were relatively new, the university chose to take advantage of these matching grant programs to construct Neils Science Center and Gellersen

Center. Federal housing programs provided low interest loans to construct the residence halls along LaPorte Avenue.

The United States entered the 1950s a changed nation. With most of Europe and Asia still trying to recover from the ruination of the war, America had become, de facto, an international economic power. Its industry and infrastructure unscathed by war, by 1951 it had successfully transitioned from a war to a consumer economy and was busily attempting to satisfy the pent-up consumer demand. Yet its inability to come to any understanding with the Soviet Union about the political organization of Europe fueled its pre-existing fear and distrust of communist governments. The idealistic promise of communism had been very attractive to segments of American society ever since the Russian revolution, and now combating communism abroad and at home became a major concern for the government. In 1947, President Harry S. Truman announced a foreign policy objective that aimed to contain the atheistic communist threat wherever it occurred in the world. In 1948 the Soviet Union challenged the United States by blocking access to Berlin, located in the Soviet sector of Germany but co-administered by the United States, England, France, and the Soviet Union. Aggressive action by the United States broke the blockade, but concern was again heightened in 1949 when the U.S.-backed Chinese government was overthrown by communist Mao Tse Tung and the Soviet Union detonated its own atom bomb. Then in 1950 the U.S. made a military response to the communist threat, entering into the civil war in Korea in support of anti-communist South Korea in its battle with communist North Korea. The United States had entered into what was to become a 40 year cold, and sometimes hot, war against the influence of the communist governments of the Soviet Union and China. This Cold War was to have profound effects on engineering education.

DEVELOPMENTS IN THE EARLY 1950S

In June, 1951, Valparaiso University awarded the first engineering degrees since 1940 to 51 graduates. By January, 1952, Kroencke Hall was ready for classes and the pressure for engineering classrooms was reduced, but the general drafting room remained in the essentially-condemned Engineering Building. By 1953 enrollment, despite the negative impact of the Korean War and the termination of the GI Bill, had risen again to near 1700 for the university, and engineering enrollment was sufficient to support a faculty of 10. Much of the energy of this enlarged faculty went into providing the much needed additional laboratory equipment and furnishings for the new Engineering Laboratory. The college was off to a good start and it was now time to build on its initial success.

In 1953 the college embarked on an interesting experiment in providing employment opportunities for engineering students. Paul H. Brandt, a 1933 Valparaiso engineering graduate, president of the A. Brandt Furniture Company of Fort Worth, Texas, and newly elected chairman of the Valparaiso board of directors, established a branch of his company in Valparaiso as a separate corporation called Branco. The university purchased a factory building on Indiana Avenue recently vacated by the local McGill Manufacturing Company and leased it to Branco to manufacture the patio furniture segment of the Ranch Oak line of furniture which Brandt had designed in the late 1930s. Dean Hesse served as its president. However, because of poor quality work by unskilled students, this experiment had a short life and by 1956 the university had to finish paying for an unused building. It was finally put to use as a central university storeroom. The Ranch Oak line has not been manufactured since 1988 when Paul Brandt closed the business, but it remains sought after in the antique furniture market.

Two significant university building projects were initiated in this period. In 1951 students had voted to assess themselves every semester to build up a fund to construct a real student union to replace the store-front space at College and Freeman Streets. This commitment was another Venture of Faith on the part of students. They believed that the project was so important to their school that they would contribute to it, even though they would never get to use it during their student days. Planning began almost immediately, and in 1953 the New York firm of Hare and Hatch was selected to design the building and a construction completion date was set for spring 1955. At the same time, with enrollment again rising, quality housing for students became a critical problem. The three war-surplus dormitories, erected in 1947 and called A, B, and C, were the only housing for upper classmen. By 1953 they were becoming impossible to heat adequately and were beginning to settle unevenly. Since the administration saw these dorms as creating morale problems (men were moving out and seeking any kind of housing that they could find in the community), new housing for men became a critical need. For a year the board struggled to find the money to attack the problem. Cleary, the situation called for another Venture of Faith. Late in 1954, with the new union building under construction, the Hare and Hatch firm was hired to design a pair of inexpensive limited-lifetime dormitories called Dau and Kreinheder, one to be completed in time for the opening of classes in September, 1955, and the other six weeks later. All three buildings were financed with 100% borrowing against the income that the rent and union assessment would produce.

THE COLLEGE SUBMITS ITS PROGRAMS TO ECPD FOR ACCREDITATION

While the university was struggling to build three buildings it had no money to pay for and continuing to experience shortfalls in operating income, the college of engineering was moving forward in its goal to achieve accreditation by the Engineers Council for Professional Development (ECPD). Accreditation was essential for its Lutheran constituency to accept the university. After a visit to Ohio Northern University, a school very similar to Valparaiso that had recently received accreditation, the college of engineering confidently submitted its application to ECPD in 1955. After the ECPD on-campus visit in May, 1955, Dean Hesse and the faculty expected a positive evaluation. Finally, in November the much anticipated ECPD report was received. The stunning action by ECPD was NOT TO ACCREDIT.

The three page report was highly complimentary about the dedication of the faculty and what it had accomplished in the six years since the start of the programs. But it found faculty salaries and capital support to be inadequate and in need of significant improvement. It indicated an understanding of the severe financial difficulties faced by the university but noted that the current fund-raising campaign "Building for Christ" gave promise of improving the financial condition of the university.

While the inadequate financial support of the college was a serious deficiency, it was the academic deficiency noted on page three that sealed the decision. As part of the accreditation procedure, departments and faculty that support the engineering program are also visited, and the combined department of physics and mathematics came in for a scathing evaluation. It began with, "The situation in physics is particularly bad in practically all aspects." After describing both the poor physical condition and housekeeping of the physics labs and offices, the report summed up its observations with, "Best description — an academic slum." After criticizing the administration for its lack of support for the department, the evaluators concluded, "In a word – the present physics situation is sterile and unpromising." The entire ECPD report concluded with this summary: "The low level of financial support for the engineering staff and its program should be remedied. The physics situation needs thorough rehabilitation as a natural science adjunct to engineering education. These constitute the debit side of the picture. On the credit side is the long and hard work of a small devoted staff which has produced acceptable curricula, acceptable courses, and acceptable laboratories in student produced space and this work cannot be too highly praised."

HERMAN C. HESSE
Herman Hesse was born March 27, 1900, in New York City. In 1918, he began work as a designer/draftsman at the Singer Manufacturing Company plant at Elizabethport, New Jersey. While working at Singer, he attended classes at the Newark Technical School, a non-degree-granting school that taught science, mathematics, and drafting. In 1920 it expanded its offerings to include cooperative programs leading to engineering degrees. In 1923 he became a full-time student, graduating in 1925, with a Bachelor of Science in Mechanical Engineering. He returned to work at Singer as a production engineer. Two years later he was awarded the Mechanical Engineer diploma, at that time a common recognition given by colleges to graduates with sufficient professional experience who submit an acceptable thesis. From 1928 to 1931 he served as assistant professor of mechanical engineering at the Newark Technical School. In 1930, the school

After the initial shock and chagrin wore off, Dean Hesse and the faculty immediately began work to find a way forward. A committee formulated proposals for action and presented them to President Kretzmann a week later. The recommendations were:
1) To create separate departments for mathematics and physics; 2) To obtain two new faculty for Physics and appoint one of them as head; 3) To revise the physics curriculum immediately; 4) To increase the capital budgets for physics and engineering; 5) To increase engineering faculty salaries; 6) To contract for the design of a new science building; 7) To rehabilitate the present science laboratories and offices for use until a new science building is complete.

Dean Hesse and Professor Kruger traveled to the University of Kentucky to review them with Professor Crouse, the regional director of ECPD. Without putting anything in writing, he indicated that if the plans as presented were executed, the chances for a favorable review were good. Acting on this information, Dean Hesse presented them at the February, 1956, board meeting. After considerable discussion of options the board voted to "authorize the Administration to make such changes and spend such sum of money as are necessary to effect accreditation immediately." Some expressed hope that prompt action in 45 days could reverse the decision, but wiser heads soon realized that the best course of action was

> changed its name to the Newark College of Engineering and is the original unit of what is now the New Jersey Institute of Technology.
>
> In 1931 he was appointed assistant professor of engineering drawing at the University of Virginia and was promoted to professor of engineering drawing and design in 1942. From 1945 to 1947 he left the academic world to become the chief engineer of the Mixing Equipment Company of Rochester, New York, but returned in 1947 as professor of mechanical engineering at the Illinois Institute of Technology in Chicago. On January 23, 1949, he accepted the appointment to be the re-founding dean of the College of Engineering at Valparaiso University. It is generally accepted college lore that George Reuss, an instructor at Valparaiso who had been Dean Hesse's student at the University of Virginia, was responsible for recommending that he be considered for the position. He officially began his duties in September, 1949, and continued until 1965 when he became
>
> *Continued next page*

to act promptly on the recommendations and re-apply to ECPD at a later date.

President Kretzmann moved quickly to find and employ two Ph.D. physicists, Armin Manning and Manuel Bretscher, both of whom were well-connected with the Lutheran Church and professionally with the Atomic Energy Commission. The abrupt manner in which physics head Ancel Thomas was relieved of his responsibility did not sit well with the faculty of the physics and mathematics department. The physicists resigned in protest. Equally quickly, plans were developed to rehabilitate the science building and during the summer of 1956, $67,000 was spent on new furniture, redecoration, and creation of new laboratory and office spaces by relocation of the boiler to the Arts-Law building. The new faculty moved quickly and by late 1957 they had obtained an Atomic Energy Commission loan of the uranium and plutonium necessary to build a sub-critical nuclear reactor. In just a few years the offerings in physics had been transformed and many engineering students were able to take electives in modern and nuclear physics.

Even before learning of the denial of accreditation, Dean Hesse had decided to address the drafting room problem. The drafting facilities had been relocated to the Foundry Annex of the Engineering Building. Kroencke Hall solved most of the classroom needs but did nothing about drafting rooms. In October, 1955, he presented the faculty with a plan

---

dean emeritus. In 1967, he was named a Distinguished Service Professor and remained an active member of the faculty until his death on November 24, 1972.

Dean Hesse was the author of three textbooks: *Engineering Tools and Processes* (1941), *A Manual in Engineering Drawing* (1942) and, with J. H. Rushton, *Process Equipment Design* (1945). In 1955 his alma mater named him "Alumnus of the Year" and in 1961 awarded him an honorary doctorate. Valparaiso named him an "Honorary Alumnus" in 1964. He was particularly proud of his membership in Tau Beta Pi. At Valparaiso he taught the engineering drawing courses and machine design and was actively involved in university governance and community affairs. In later years he added thespian to his list of accomplishments, acting in various roles in productions of the Valparaiso Community Theater Guild. Herman and his wife Helen had no children. They were generous benefactors of the College of Engineering and Valparaiso University.

drawn by architect Paul Tanck to construct a 4000 square foot building in two phases directly east of the Engineering Laboratory for drafting rooms. Paul Tanck was a partner with civil engineering professor Charles Peller in a local architectural and engineering firm. By spring this plan had become a 6200 square foot classroom and drafting room building. To help pay for it, Dean Hesse and his wife, Helen, provided $30,000 for a "Deferred Income Gift Certificate" annuity, the proceeds of which were used toward its construction. In June, 1956, construction was approved by the board. The complete cost of the building was $62,450, about $10.00 per square foot. It contained large and mid-sized drafting rooms, two classrooms, offices for the Dean of Engineering, a room for the engineering supply store, and one other office. Combining two family names, it was called Graland Hall after Helen Hesse's parents George Grafe and Barbara Oland Grafe. With the completion of this building the college was finally able to leave behind the several-times-condemned Engineering Building.

The Start of the Revolution in Engineering Education

Two events in the mid-1950s had revolutionary impact on engineering education. The first was the "Report of the Committee on Evaluation of Engineering Education," released in the summer of 1955 and generally known as the Grinter Report after the chairman of the committee, Linton E. Grinter. The study was done by the American Society for Engineering Education (the name of SPEE after 1946) at the request of ECPD in its role as the representative of the engineering profession. Its major conclusion was that the science and engineering science content of engineering curricula needed upgrading at the expense of engineering practice. The second event was the Soviet Union's successful launch of its scientific satellite, Sputnik I, on October 4, 1957.

The impact of the Grinter Report in many ways positioned engineering education to participate in the national response to the Sputnik challenge. The engineering profession was chagrined to realize that it had made only secondary contributions to the technological innovations spawned by the war effort. Curricular emphasis on current practice had ill

Graland Hall

prepared engineers in the fundamental and engineering sciences on which the new developments were based. The opening paragraph of the Grinter Report is quite clear about the direction for the future. "Engineering Education must contribute to the development of men who can face new and difficult engineering situations with imagination and competence. Meeting such situations invariably involves both professional and social responsibilities. The Committee considers that *scientifically oriented engineering curricula* (italics added) are essential to achieve these ends and recommends the following means of implementation." It then followed with 10 recommendations:

> 1) Strengthen the work in the basic sciences of mathematics, chemistry, and physics; 2) Emphasize the common core of six engineering sciences; 3) Base engineering analysis, design, and systems on the core of basic and engineering sciences; 4) Include elective courses to develop the special talents of individual students; 5) Strengthen the work in humanistic studies and social sciences; 6) Insist on high level performance in oral, written, and graphical communication; 7) Strengthen graduate programs; 8) Take steps to train and recruit faculty who can teach this scientifically-based curriculum; 9) Encourage curricular experiments; 10) Make these changes as quickly as possible.

These recommendations were developed in great detail for both undergraduate and graduate programs. For the most part they were stated in positive terms, but a few of the negative observations give some insight into the conditions professional leaders were trying to change. The following three quotations suggest an overview of such comments. "The major department sequences in many instances are dull and uninspiring, utilizing practices long outdated." "Shop courses and all other courses emphasizing practical work that tend to displace engineering sciences … should be scrutinized critically." "Some attention to engineering art and practice is necessary, but its high purpose is to illuminate the engineering science, analysis, or design, rather than to teach the art as engineering methodology." The report recommended approximate time allocations to each of the major portions of an engineering curriculum: mathematics and basic science, about 25%; engineering sciences, about 25%; engineering analysis, design and necessary technological background, about 25%; humanities and social sciences, about 20%; and electives, about 10%. The report noted that this allocation added up to more than 100% and suggested that there will be many reasons for variations among departments and institutions.

Draft forms of the study were widely distributed for comment from the professional societies that made up ECPD, from engineering educators, and from the physics and mathematics community. It received financial support from the Engineering Foundation, the constituent societies of ECPD, and the National Science Foundation. It was a clear exposition of "marching orders" to any engineering program that desired accreditation from ECPD. The final distribution requirements as stated by ECPD in its 1958 accreditation guidelines varied only slightly from the study's recommendations. Stated in years instead of percentages, they were one year of math and science, one year of engineering science, one-half year of engineering analysis and design, and one-half to one year of humanities and social science. The remaining time for electives and engineering technology background was left to the discretion of the institution.

The second event to have a significant impact on engineering education was the Soviet Union's successful launch of a rocket to put its Sputnik scientific satellite in orbit in 1957. It ended any complacency about the superiority of American technology. The U.S. attempts to launch its own satellite in the same year had all ended in rocket failures. When the Soviet Union had demonstrated its own atomic bomb in 1949, Americans had assumed that it was the result of Soviet espionage. Soviet tests of a fission-fusion bomb in 1953 and a true hydrogen bomb in 1955 had been troubling signs that American superiority was being challenged. With the launch of Sputnik no doubt remained about the challenge. Improved education was seen as central to the response. In less than a year Congress passed the National Defense Education Act, thus moving the federal government into the mainstream of support for education. To encourage more college enrollment, it provided low cost student loans as well as financial support for institutions to improve programs in science, mathematics, and modern foreign languages. Soon the National Science Foundation and the Defense Department were providing significant support for graduate students and research in sciences, engineering, and mathematics. Low cost loans and grant programs for facilities construction followed in 1963. The 1955 Grinter Report, with its call for increased science content in the curriculum, had positioned engineering education to participate in this dynamic shift in national priorities.

Mechanical Engineering Heat Power Lab

Accreditation is Achieved

The decade of the 1950s was a significant growth period for both the College of Engineering and Valparaiso University. Total undergraduate and engineering enrollment grew steadily from 1624 and 247 in 1951 to 2488 and 402 in 1959. As a result of the fund drive conducted among congregations in the Missouri Synod, Valparaiso received $2,250,000 to retire debt and to build the Chapel of the Resurrection. Ground was broken in September, 1956, just two months before a fire destroyed the 1893 Auditorium Building. The fact that the library, immediately north of the auditorium, was even more vulnerable to fire and also could have been lost, once again caused planning to shift from building a new administration building to planning for a new library. Grants totaling $250,000 from the Lilly Endowment and a gift from Margaret Moellering of $375,000 enabled the start of construction on the new library in 1958. Moellering Library was completed in 1959. (When analysis showed that it could not effectively be retrofitted as part of a new student union, it was razed in 2005 to make room for the Harrre Union.) These new buildings filled major university needs, but it seemed that the housing crunch of the post-war years was now being repeated 10 years later. With more than 800 new students expected for the 1956-57 school year, including 180 freshman engineers, the administration began to pursue financing for a new dormitory through loans from the Federal Housing Authority. After some initial difficulty with obtaining the loan, in 1958 construction was begun on Wehrenberg Hall at the east end of the campus.

With the improvement of both physical facilities and financial support for engineering and physics, a general improvement in the university finances, and the new construction that was under way, a new request to ECPD for accreditation was submitted in 1958. The news in October that all three programs had been accredited for a three-year period was met with great relief, excitement, and celebration. Ten years after the Venture of Faith, the hard work of the faculty and administration had finally been validated. At the review in 1961, the College of Engineering was accredited for the maximum five-year term.

Fluid Mechanics Laboratory

Building on Success

Dean Hesse, fearing that university faculty governance might be limited to deans and department heads, created a departmental organization for the College of Engineering in 1957. Previously the dean had been the only official administrative officer; now Charles Peller, William Shewan, and Fred Kruger were named heads of civil, electrical, and mechanical engineering, giving them titles that reflected their actual work. Now that ECPD recognition had been achieved, the dean and department heads could move their focus to building quality in faculty, students, curricula, and programs.

Two programs to foster faculty and student research were begun in 1960. Under the direction of Professor Leslie Zoss, the college initiated an Industrial Research and Development program, the objective of which was to give aid to area industry on a research contract basis. The benefit to Valparaiso was to be in money and equipment to support faculty-student research that could not otherwise be justified in an undergraduate program. To support this effort, the mechanical engineering department introduced a required two-semester senior course for a total of three credits titled "Engineering Systems Analysis," and selected seniors worked on these supported projects. Research proposals were solicited from area industries. This course was the prototype for the senior project courses that have become one of the hallmarks of the Valparaiso engineering curriculum in all three departments. Over time the mechanical engineering department had better success than the other departments in attracting industry-supported projects. In civil engineering, Professor A. Sami El-Naggar, who joined the faculty in 1960 as the second member to have an earned doctorate in engineering, began a research program in environmental engineering supported by a grant from the National Science Foundation. He also developed an air-quality monitoring system for the Porter County government. Both these research programs involved students as research assistants.

Dean Hesse prepared a 10-year plan in 1961 which had these objectives: to begin a Master of Engineering degree program by 1970; to add an industrial engineering degree by 1965 and an architectural engineering degree by 1970; to construct four "Graland Hall" buildings, one for each degree program, on the east campus by 1970; to develop a computer center supervised by the department of mathematics; and to appoint an assistant dean in 1963 to serve for two years and become dean when Dean Hesse stepped down at age 65. While not a explicit part of Dean Hesse's 10-year plan, building a stronger, stable faculty was also one of his objectives. By 1960 the faculty of 18 included 13 who would spend the rest of their academic careers at Valparaiso University. These 13 were: Fred Kruger, Herman Hesse, Charles Peller, Kenneth Mortimer, William Shewan, Edgar Luecke, Merlyn Vocke, Gilbert Lehmann, Gerhard Vater, Robert Isbell, Leslie Zoss, A. Sami El-Naggar, and James Schueler. In the early 1960s Professors Shewan, Lehmann, Luecke, and Vocke took leaves of varying lengths to complete graduate work for doctorates in engineering. In future years, Kruger, Lehmann, Shewan and Luecke were to serve as deans of the college.

For students, accreditation provided several opportunities for professional involvement and recognition. Graduates were now permitted to sit for the first portion of the professional licensing exam during their senior year instead of having to first achieve three years of engineering experience. The professional engineering societies would now sponsor student chapters, and chapters of the American Society of Civil Engineers and the American Society of Mechanical Engineers were established. Not so restrictive, the Institute of Radio Engineers had sponsored a student chapter at Valparaiso in the early 1950s. This student chapter became a part of the Institute of Electrical and Electronics Engineers when the Institute of Radio Engineers merged with the American Institute of Electrical Engineers. With the objective of achieving membership in Tau Beta Pi, the Appian Society was established in 1959 with graduating senior James Schueler as president. The society was named for Appius Claudius, famous for his public works in 4th century B.C. Rome. In 1963 it became the Indiana Delta chapter of Tau Beta Pi with future dean Stuart Walesh as president.

Curriculum Development

Until 1958 the engineering curriculum was essentially unchanged from the one established in 1948. Credits required for graduation in civil engineering decreased from 154 to 151; in electrical they remained unchanged at 152; mechanical dropped from 151 to 146. The physical education requirement was reduced from 4 to 2 credits. The first two years remained common for all three degrees except for the beginning course in each major in the fourth semester. The civil engineers were required to take a seven week, eight hours per day, 5 days per week summer surveying camp for which they received 6 credits. Small changes were made nearly every year following accreditation in 1958. The credits required for graduation settled down to the mid 140s.

The impact of a new physics faculty and the recommendations of the Grinter Report began to show up in 1958: that year the curriculum required that engineers take the same physics course as physics majors, but the next year a special 10 credit course for engineers was instituted. Also in 1959 the mathematics sequence was upgraded to start calculus in the second semester in a three-course sequence that included analytic geometry. Nuclear physics was required in the EE program in 1957. This

Electrical Machinery Laboratory with Professor Merlyn Vocke

was changed to modern physics in 1959. In response to the Grinter Report recommendation to allow students to take more electives so that they could tailor their program to their career objectives, in 1959 a moderate list of electives that included courses in the major or advanced math or physics was made available. In CE the 6 credit summer camp in surveying was changed to 3 credits during the school year and 3 credits of summer camp in 1958, and by 1962 the summer camp was eliminated. Courses in water supply and sewerage and in advanced sanitary engineering were added in 1960. Required courses in electromagnetic field theory, servomechanisms, and information theory were added to the EE program. The ME curriculum added required courses in heat transfer and vibrations and offered the senior project "Engineering System Analysis" course as an elective. Most of these changes reflected an added emphasis on engineering science.

The first mention of computers occurred in 1959 when a course called "Computers" was required in the EE curriculum, concentrating on analog computers and on the basics of digital computer circuits. Electronic analog computers had been developed in the 1940s to solve the differential equations at the heart of dynamic systems, and at the time were seen as the only practical way to simulate these systems. The university acquired an IBM 610 computer, a small vacuum tube machine that could be operated by one person in an uncontrolled environment, and the mathematics department offered its first digital computer-based courses in numerical analysis in 1960. In 1962 the IBM 610 was replaced by the IBM 1620, a machine designed for scientific and engineering applications that used resistor-transistor logic and paper-tape input and output. The following year the mathematics department offered a course for engineering and business students in the FORTRAN, ALGOL, and COBAL languages. Realizing the growing importance of electronic computers, in 1962 the ME department instituted a course in digital and analog methods which was then also required of CE students. Finally in 1965 the 1959 EE computer course and the 1962 ME course were merged into a general computer methods course required of all engineering students. The IBM 1620 was upgraded to punched card input and typed paper output in 1968.

By far the most significant curricular change occurred in 1964. The new physics faculty installed in 1956 rather quickly improved both the quality of the introductory physics course and the expectations for student performance. Coincidently, the success rate for engineering students in the physics course declined. Not surprisingly, this became a seriously contentious issue between the physics department and the engineering college. In memos to the vice president for academic affairs during the summer of 1963, Dean Hesse stated his concerns about the grades that the engineers had earned in the physics course during the academic year just completed. He pointed out that during the fall semester only 55% of the 94 students were awarded grades of C or better. What was even worse, only 52% of the survivors of the first semester course earned grades of C or better the second semester. In addition, he was distressed by the fact that each year several promising engineering students transferred their major to physics after beginning the physics course. Dean Hesse concluded one memo with the observation, "We in the College of Engineering have been struggling with the problem of low grades in our service courses in Physics for six years; our protests do not seem to have been effective." The dispute escalated all the way to

President Kretzmann's office. Unable to broker a satisfactory solution to the dispute, President Kretzmann summarily ended a meeting by announcing that the college of engineering would henceforth teach its own physics course. The subject matter and credits in mechanics, heat, and electricity were absorbed into the existing engineering science courses and two special courses were added in wave motion and modern physics. This unfortunate divorce lasted until 1992.

Dean Hesse's 10-year plan had called for starting a graduate program, and the faculty went right to work on the proposal. In April, 1962, a preliminary report found that prospects to obtain support from regional industry were not promising. In 1965 the study was re-activated in light of the ASEE/ECPD "Goals of Engineering" study, currently in development, that recommended a Master's degree as the first professional engineering degree. Faculty visited a number of smaller engineering schools with graduate programs, developed a potential curriculum, and made a cost estimate. The committee concluded that a graduate program, to start in 1967, was feasible. However, the proposal was never acted on.

Notable Students from the 1950s and 1960s

Enrollment in the college grew steadily from 247 in 1951 to a peak of 457 in 1957 and then leveled off to around 400 for the next ten years. From a low of 32 in 1954, graduates reached a peak of 74 in 1958 and then averaged around 60. Though from time to time women enrolled in the college, until 1956 none had graduated since the McCall sisters in 1915. Showing that women could excel in engineering, Kathryn Sandborg graduated first in her mechanical engineering class in 1956. The other women graduates in this era were: Barbara Schultz, EE '57; Carol Hild and Marilyn Moeller, ME '58; and Ruth Klopp, EE '60. For the next ten years there were none. In 1959 Kinsey Baker Brown, the grandson of founder Henry Baker Brown, graduated in mechanical engineering. In the six consecutive years from 1964 to 1969, a senior received a prestigious Tau Beta Pi Fellowship for graduate study. At the time, no other engineering college in the country had matched that record.

Many graduates from this era have had distinguished careers in engineering and business. After their graduation some kept strong ties to the college and university, giving back their time, talent, and wealth. Future faculty members were: Merlyn Vocke, EE '55; Edgar Luecke, EE '55; Gilbert Lehmann, ME '55; Henry Jud, EE '56; Anatol Longinow, CE '58; James Schueler, CE '59; Demos Gelopulos, EE '60; Dale Kempf, EE '62; Stuart Walesh, CE '63; William Schoech, EE '66; and John Steffen, ME '66. Future members of the university board of directors were: Howard Claussen, ME '55; Donald Fites, CE '56; Alger Meitz, EE '58; Richard Beumer, EE '59; Gerald Pelzer, CE '60, serving for a number of years as chairman, and Stephen Furbacher, ME '70. Members of the National Council for the College of Engineering were: Edward Tornberg, EE '55; Eugene Holland, CE '57; Ralph Johnson, CE '59; John Draheim, EE '64; John Yakimow, ME '64; Roger Sims, CE '65; James Beyreis, CE '66; T. C. Schwan, Jr., ME '66, and Stephen Furbacher, ME '70. Ron Zech, EE '65 was a member of the National Council for the College of Business Administration.

The endowment to support the Jenny Professorship of Emerging Technology was established by his family to honor Frederick F. Jenny, EE '56, who held chief executive positions with several Unisys Corporation subsidiaries. In various ways he used his influence in support of the college and university, including arranging for the initial introduction of

FRED WALTER KRUGER

Fred Kruger served Valparaiso University as teacher, mechanical engineering department head, dean of engineering, and vice president for business affairs. He was born on December 17, 1921, in Chicago. Recognizing his potential, both his mother and pastor encouraged him to attend Valparaiso to study engineering after graduating from Tilden Tech in Chicago. He enrolled in 1940 to start the joint program with Purdue. While at Purdue he joined the Naval Reserve and graduated with a B.S.E.E in 1943. From Purdue he was sent to the United States Naval Academy in Annapolis, Maryland, for more training and then was assigned to the newly launched USS Saginaw Bay, an escort aircraft carrier in the Pacific theater of the war, as an engineering officer in charge of the engine room.

His experience in the engine room sparked his life-long interest in

word-processing computers for student use in the academic computer center.

THE GELLERSEN ENGINEERING AND MATHEMATICS CENTER

Although it must have seemed impossible to the board and administration only a few years earlier, a building boom hit the campus in 1960. From 1955 to 1966, undergraduate enrollment increased from 2180 to 3246. Construction of Dau, Kreinheder, and Wehrenberg residence halls provided only a brief respite in the demand for quality student housing. In short order, four residence halls along LaPorte Avenue were completed: Scheele in 1961, Brandt in 1962, Lankenau in 1964, and Alumni in 1966. These were all financed with low interest loans from the federal government, which was responding to burgeoning college enrollments throughout the country. Scheele was designed to house the sororities which had been living in substandard converted old homes scattered about the old campus. When this building program was completed, Lembke Hall was converted to faculty offices and Altruria Hall and Dodge Hall were closed and sold. Only the fraternities remained in poor housing in the old campus area, and planning was underway to move them to new buildings on Mound Street. In addition to these new dorms, the Lutheran Deaconess Association had

---

thermodynamics. When he completed his Navy service, he returned to Purdue to study thermodynamics and earned a B.S.M.E. degree in 1947. In August 1947 he began a 42 year career at Valparaiso. When College of Engineering department heads were established in 1957, he became the first head of mechanical engineering. After serving as associate dean and then acting dean during the illness of Dean Hesse, he was named dean in 1966. He returned to the engineering faculty in 1972 for two years before being appointed as vice president of business affairs, a position he held until his retirement in 1986. For a few years after retirement, he taught thermodynamics courses part time and could be found prowling the halls of Gellersen and the machine shop, where he was working on projects, until his final illness.

Dean Kruger was very active in Valparaiso city government. For 32 years he was elected to the Valparaiso City Council as a Republican and for many of those years served as its president. He died on December 25, 2006, at the age of 85.

constructed Deaconess Hall (now Huegli Hall) on leased land to serve as the residence and program center for students enrolled in its training program.

Thirty years of painstaking development work by Karl Henrichs bore fruit in the 1960s with the receipt of three significant gifts. A bequest from the trust established by Adolph Wesemann, along with other fund-raising efforts, was used to construct the first Wesemann Hall (now Kretzmann Hall) in 1964 to house the School of Law. This trust ultimately yielded $3,000,000 to the university. Gifts totaling $1,000,000 in honor of Mary and Julius Neils by their 13 children put the planning for new science labs and classrooms on the fast track. In January, 1964, architect Edward Stade was commissioned to "provide at once" plans for the first unit of a science building at an anticipated cost of $1,200,000. To augment the Neils money, the university applied for a grant from the federal government under the January, 1963, Higher Education Facilities Act (HEFC). This program was to run for five years and provide outright grants of one-third of the construction cost in addition to low interest loans for the construction of science, mathematics, and modern foreign languages facilities. Engineering was included under the science category. Since the physics labs had been updated in 1956, it was decided that the first unit of Neils Science Center would consist of labs and offices for biology and chemistry. Detailed planning resulted in the cost increasing to about $1,500,000, of which the HEFC grant covered $500,000. This first wing was dedicated in 1966. In addition to these major structures, the period also saw the first addition to Hilltop Gymnasium, expansion of the Valparaiso Union to include a bookstore, a building (now Heidbrink Hall) to house the admissions and financial aid operation, and Loke Hall for the home economics program.

The third large bequest was realized late in 1964, about $1,000,000 from the estate of William Gellersen of Oakland, California. President Kretzmann's proposal to the board in October to use the money to finally build an administration building did not meet with enthusiasm from the academic administrators. They were acutely aware of the need for classrooms. In response to their concerns, Kretzmann created a committee on facilities composed of members of his administrative council. In January, 1965, the executive committee of the board approved that committee's recommendation to use $700,000 from the Gellersen money for a classroom building, with the remaining $300,000 to be kept in a reserve. Professor Fred Kruger, who had been named associate dean of engineering in 1964 and was serving as acting dean during the illness of Dean Hesse, proposed a plan to use the Gellersen money, augmented with a one-third HEFC grant, to construct two buildings, one for modern foreign languages and the other to be shared by mathematics and engineering. This plan was unanimously recommended to the board by its committee on facilities at its May, 1965, meeting.

The details of the plan were as follows: increase the Gellersen estate allocation to $950,000; construct a $500,000 building for classrooms, offices, and language laboratories for foreign language, and classrooms for biology and chemistry; construct a $900,000 building for offices, classrooms, and a computer laboratory for mathematics and classrooms, offices and laboratories for engineering. Of this $900,000, $600,000 would be allocated to the engineering portion of the building. Detailed planning began immediately. The board reviewed preliminary plans at its August meeting and authorized applications for two HEFA grants based on building costs of $850,000 and $500,000. Initial thoughts on location placed Gellersen on the north side of the campus road southeast of the new Neils Science Center and Meier Hall southeast of the Valparaiso Union. Planners soon realized that the lack of nearby utilities made the Meier Hall site untenable and the location was changed to be adjacent to Gellersen. Since poor subsoil conditions on the north side of the road threatened to add significantly to the construction cost, the location of both buildings was then moved to the south side of the road. As often happens in building projects, when bids were opened in August, 1966, Gellersen was 37% over budget at $1,166,000 and Meier 22% at $610,000. When the money already spent in planning plus a contingency of 2% were added in, the total project costs were $1,306,000 for Gellersen and $780,000 for Meier. The $25 per square foot cost of Gellersen, when compared to costs for the earlier engineering buildings, reflected both better quality and inflated construction costs.

The executive committee of the board met on September 9, 1966, in Chicago to consider the options. Fred Kruger, now dean of the college, presented a written report to the board, outlining the options: 1) reject the bids and forfeit $577,000 in grants; 2) build one building and forfeit the grant for the other; or 3) accept the bids and arrange the added financing with increased grants and a 3%, 50-year loan from Title III of the HEFA program. Dean Kruger pointed out that the full project would add 24 general classrooms and more than 50 faculty offices to the university inventory of facilities. After some discussion, motions to authorize the request for grants and borrowing for each project and to accept the construction bids were offered and passed. Previously prepared "notices to proceed" were immediately sent to the winning bidders. The new home for the College of Engineering was underway.

Gellersen Engineering and Mathematics Center was essentially completed in January, 1968. With the decision to get as much building as possible for the funds available, the laboratories were literally nothing more than four blank walls, since no laboratory furniture or equipment was included in the construction program. Conduits to distribute electrical power to the laboratories were empty. Throughout the spring semester as individual pieces of equipment were no longer needed for instruction, they were moved to the new building. Some lab furniture that had been left behind when the chemistry and biology labs were moved to Neils Science Center was appropriated for use until

WILLIAM HENRY AUGUST GELLERSEN
The construction of the Gellersen Engineering and Mathematics Center was made possible by the approximately $1,000,000 unrestricted estate gift of William Gellersen. When it was received in 1964, it was the largest gift in the history of Valparaiso University. Gellersen's connection to Valparaiso University was tenuous at best; apparently his only visit to the campus was in October, 1963, less than a year before his death. His interest in Valparaiso was stimulated by his boyhood friends at the one-room Lutheran parochial school he attended in what is now Hillside, Illinois. Three of them, all friends of Valparaiso, were William Boeger, a member of the university board of directors, and successful attorneys Adolph Wesemann and Edward Seegers. Wesemann's gift built the first Wesemann Hall and Seegers endowed the Seegers Chair in Law.

new lab furniture could be obtained. Formal dedication ceremonies were held on November 2 and 3, 1968, with afternoon invited academic lectures and a banquet on Saturday evening at which James Beggs, an administrator at NASA, was the featured speaker. At the Sunday dedicatory convocation, Dean Richard Baepler of Christ College, which had been established two years earlier, was the preacher.

Space left behind in the Engineering Laboratory Building was appropriated by the music and art departments for offices, rehearsal rooms, individual practice rooms, and art studios. The building was renamed Art-Music. With the 1997 construction of the Center for the Arts, the psychology department relocated from Engineering Annex/Moody Hall to the space vacated by the music department and the building was renamed Art-Psychology. Graland Hall was reworked to serve as offices and work spaces for what is now the Office of Institutional Advancement.

Engineering Education in the 1960s

By 1960 the almost-radical reconfiguration of engineering education to a science-based curriculum was firmly established, but not without a reaction from those who favored practice-based education. As engineering colleges de-emphasized practice, industry began to lobby

---

Thirty years of quiet cultivation by Karl Henrichs and the example of his friends convinced him to leave the bulk of his estate to Valparaiso University.

Much of what we know of William Gellersen comes from a copy in the university archive of the eulogy given by Reverend Alfred Koehler at his funeral on September 3, 1964, in Oakland, California. He was born on May 2, 1880, on a farm in Dundee, Kane County, near Elgin, Illinois. His parents, both born in 1853, had emigrated from Germany. His father was of Danish background. He had an older sister and a younger brother. When he was 6 years old, his father was killed in a farming accident. In 1889 his mother married a widower with 9 children and relocated to Proviso Township in Cook County. There he attended Immanuel Lutheran School, where instruction was surely primarily in German, and then the local public township school for the upper grades. After his Confirmation at Immanuel, at the age of 13 he went to work on his step-father's farm. With much

Continued next page

for the creation of four-year courses that brought practice back into the curriculum. Colleges and universities responded with enthusiasm by developing technology courses that mirrored standard engineering curricula but with an emphasis on practice instead of theory. In many cases the course titles and descriptions were indistinguishable between the two. In order to clearly define the differences, in 1965 ECPD announced its intention to develop criteria for accrediting four-year programs in engineering technology. (Precedents for establishing criteria and procedures for accreditation of technology programs had been established in the mid-1940s when ECPD offered accreditation for two-year technician courses.) The first engineering technology degrees were accredited in 1967. In its role of representing the engineering profession to the general public, ECPD prominently presented definitions of Engineering and Engineering Technology in its 1967 annual report: "Engineering is the profession in which a knowledge of the mathematical and natural sciences gained by study, experience, and practice is applied with judgment to develop ways to utilize, economically, the materials and forces of nature for the benefit of mankind. Engineering Technology is that part of the technological field which requires the application of scientific and engineering knowledge and methods combined with technical skills in support of engineering activities; it lies in the occupational spectrum between the craftsman and the engineer at the end of the spectrum closest to the engineer." The terms "engineering technician" and "engineering technologist"

---

encouragement from his mother, at sixteen he enrolled in the Chicago Business College where he struggled, perhaps because of poor skill in English, but persevered. This was the extent of his formal education. After a year's work in the office at the Webber Wagon Company, he quit when he was not given the raise in salary that he felt he deserved. Then at the age of 19 he began his life-long career with the Libby, McNeill, Libby Company in its Chicago purchasing department.

At the age of 23, he relocated as a bookkeeper to the first west coast office of Libby at San Francisco. His talent was recognized and he was promoted to branch manager of the Portland, Oregon, office in 1910. In 1916 he returned to San Francisco and was named the general sales manager in that office in 1919. He became general manager of sales and promotion for the entire west coast division in 1923. He remained in sales for the rest of his career, and at his retirement in 1945 he was vice president and general manager of the west

were recommended to describe graduates of two-year and four-year technology programs.

With the sudden prominence of science and engineering in the national priorities brought on by the Cold War and the post-Sputnik space race, in 1961 ECPD asked ASEE to conduct another major study of the goals of engineering education. In the intervening six years after the Grinter Report, graduate education and research had grown in importance and technology programs had emerged. Eric Walker of Pennsylvania State University was chosen to lead the study which was divided into two sections, one for undergraduate education led by George Hawkins from Purdue and one for graduate education led by Joseph Petit of Stanford. As with the Grinter study, draft recommendations were widely circulated for comment, but this time several drew strong negative response. There were no real objections to recommendations for increased funding for research, development of part-time graduate programs, greater emphasis on liberal arts, and improved faculty development and recruitment. Four other recommendations, however, went to the core of the model for engineering education that had existed for a century: that the first professional degree should be the Master of Engineering; that required credits in the undergraduate curriculum should be reduced by 15%; that ECPD should accredit only Master's degrees; and that Bachelor's degrees should be accredited not by discipline but by the engineering unit as a whole. This last

> coast operations and a member of the board of Libby, McNeill, and Libby. He is generally credited with the development of the pineapple industry in Hawaii. His pastor stated in the eulogy that William Gellersen had been offered further promotion in the company but had declined for personal reasons, "among them consideration of his wife's health."
>
> In 1910 he married Mabel Carroll in San Francisco who preceded him in death in 1947. They had two sons: Richard, the elder, was killed in an auto accident in 1954; the younger died at birth. There were no grandchildren. In his will, he was generous to his extended family and close friends, but the bulk of his estate went to Valparaiso. An article in the *Oakland Tribune* titled "The Last Will of a 'Man of Modest Means' " said that his friends at the Claremont Country Club assumed that he was "comfortable but not wealthy." They were surprised when the probate court revealed that his estate was $1,500,000. Gellersen died August 31, 1964, in Oakland of an apparent heart attack.

recommendation drew particular opposition from both the electrical and chemical engineering communities, who feared that existing programs would evolve into a one-size-fits-all curriculum and fail to accommodate enough specialized undergraduate courses to make it possible to offer a viable Master's degree. The Valparaiso faculty indicated its desire to maintain a four-year first-degree program, with a separate Master's degree. It specifically rejected the proposal for an integrated five-year program that awarded a Master's as the first degree.

The final "Goals of Engineering Education" report in 1968 was unable to resolve the conflicting views and had little immediate effect. ECPD itself rejected the recommendation to accredit the engineering unit as a whole. The only movement towards making the Master's degree the first professional degree was to offer accreditation of Master's degrees in addition to the Bachelor's. Throughout the 1970s about 10% of schools requested this dual-level accreditation. Deans of large research institutions actively opposed any accreditation of graduate work as both unnecessary and harmful. By the late 1970s, under pressure from the Council of Postsecondary Accreditation, dual-level accreditation was dropped.

EIGHT

The College Matures: 1968 -1985

The completion of Gellersen Center in 1968 coincided nationally with the onset of one of the most difficult periods in American political and social history and locally with the completion of twenty-eight years of leadership by President Kretzmann. Especially for younger readers, this chapter begins with an extensive overview of national and local events and their impact on Valparaiso University. New president Albert Huegli inherited a financially weakened institution and a restive student body and faculty. He worked diligently to guide the transition to new academic and social relationships among students, faculty, and administration and to shore up the finances of the university. Instead of being able to take full advantage of the new building, the college of engineering was forced to put much of its energy into rebuilding enrollment after a significant downturn in the early 1970s. In spite of limited budgets and severe inflation that left salaries 25% below those of peer institutions, the academic quality of the faculty was improved.

The essential curricular problem was to respond to the growing impact that digital computing was having on both course content and engineering practice. In the late 1970s the university finally was able to make the transition from batch processing to time-sharing computers, just in time for the emergence of microprocessors and the personal computer. The microprocessor made it economical to include digital computing in engineered products, and the electrical engineering department began offering a wide array of computer-related courses. In 1984 the department renamed itself the electrical and computer engineering department and offered a degree called Computer Science and Engineering. In response to the severe economic recession of the early 1980s, the college instituted a cooperative education program that was intended to offer students practical experience, an advantage in a difficult employment market.

The period from 1968 to 1985 saw a significant increase in the number of engineering programs in the nation. This increase brought great pressure on ECPD to manage its accreditation activities; at the same time, accreditation criteria became more prescriptive and fewer programs received the maximum period of accreditation. To manage this situation, in 1980 ECPD was reorganized as the Accreditation Board for Engineering and Technology (ABET) with activities limited to accrediting engineering and technology programs.

The Nation

In the years leading up to 1968 both the Civil Rights Movement and the Vietnam War were causing great stress to the established order. Citizens demanded enforcement of the Civil Rights Act of 1964 and the Voting Rights Act of 1965, often in the face of active, and especially in the South, violent opposition to them by local government leaders. In the North, race riots erupted in Newark and Detroit in 1967. At the same time, the country's support of anti-communist South Vietnam changed in its level of involvement by committing combat troops in 1965. This required a rapid and drastic increase in the number of young men being drafted into the armed services, from 112,000 in 1964 to 382,000 in 1966. By 1966 anti-war protests were being organized; spurred by the heavy draft demands, their intensity increased in 1967. Added to the volatile mix was the country's reaction to the growing "counter-culture" of "sex, drugs, and rock-and-roll" embraced by the first wave of baby-boomers. By the mid-1960s oral contraceptives were becoming generally available and drug use was moving into the mainstream culture. Along with these upheavals, animosity was growing between college students and the rest of society. The privileged position and perceived counter-culture lifestyle of college men, who were deferred from the draft, made college-age students the focal point of "the establishment" reaction to the anti-war and civil rights protests. Woodstock 1969 became a defining event for the youth culture.

The eventful year of 1968 began with the January 30th offensive by the Viet Cong, a South Vietnamese rebel group seeking to reunify Vietnam under North Vietnam's communist government. While the offensive was ultimately a defeat for the rebels, its impact convinced more Americans that the war was not going as well as they had been led to believe, causing general support for the war to decline. With support for the war and his presidency at a low point, Lyndon Johnson announced at the end of March that he would not be a candidate in the upcoming election. Then on April 4, Martin Luther King was assassinated, greatly increasing existing tensions.

In the lead-up to the Indiana primary, both Democratic candidates for president, Robert Kennedy and Eugene McCarthy, appeared on the Valparaiso campus, with 5000 attending a campus rally in April for Robert Kennedy. Two months later he was shot and killed at a victory rally after the California primary election. Already battered by the assassination of two charismatic national leaders, the national conscience was further distressed over the excessive actions by police in breaking up demonstrations at the National Democratic Convention in Chicago in August. By that time more than 200 student demonstrations and protests at over 100 colleges had taken place. In a mood of distress, confusion, and anger, the nation elected Richard Nixon on the basis of his secret plan to end the war.

Valparaiso University

While the engineering faculty and students were eagerly working on the move to Gellersen for the start of the fall semester, 1968, the university was planning for its new era without O. P. Kretzmann as president. His retirement was set to begin in summer, and the board was winding up its search for his successor. In May, the board publicly announced that Norman Graebner, a nationally recognized scholar and holder of an endowed chair in history at the University of Virginia, had accepted the presidency. But within a few weeks he had second thoughts and declined the appointment. Efforts by board members to get him to reconsider failed, and the board appointed vice president Albert Huegli, who also had been a candidate for the position, as acting president. After one semester as acting president, in December he accepted their offer of the presidency. As its new leader, he took over an institution that was facing significant financial problems and growing student unrest. The financial problems resulted from the explosive construction program of the 60s coupled with an administration that did not effectively confront the growing yearly deficits. Little comfort could be taken in the fact that other universities were facing much the same problem. For a number of years into the 1970s, weak finances slowed the development of both the university and the college of engineering.

While Valparaiso University, with its more conservative Lutheran students, was not on the forefront of the revolutions taking place on campuses across the nation, it was also not immune to them. At Valparaiso the confrontation took the form of a student protest against the creation of the new position of vice president for student affairs and the appointment, without consultation, of Walter Rubke in early 1969. Believing that a promise of student involvement in the selection had not been kept, student leaders seized on this issue to form a student coalition and to send a document to President Huegli stating, "There is an acute need for greater student participation in the affairs of Valparaiso University. There are a number of areas of student life where students feel that the present university policy does not meet their needs." A reply from the president, the document stipulated, was expected by March 14, 1969. President Huegli replied, announcing that an All Campus Conference would be held on March 18 and 19. At that meeting a consensus was reached that some change in campus governance was advisable; following the meeting an ad hoc committee of 5 student leaders and 5 senior faculty members was formed to negotiate the details. The outcome was the "Instrument for Internal Governance" which created a University Senate to replace the Faculty Senate. This new senate was comprised of both faculty and student membership in a 2-1 ratio. One of the 5 faculty members on the ad hoc committee was Professor Leslie Zoss of the mechanical engineering department. Aware that the engineering faculty opposed participation of students in matters of the curriculum and professional standards, he worked effectively to maintain issues such as faculty promotion and tenure, graduation requirements, and professional school curricula under the exclusive control of the faculty.

Having won a seat at the table, students began the 1969-1970 year working to effect changes in residence hall policies and academic programs. They soon became frustrated with the slow progress, since both the administration and faculty were not in agreement with their more radical proposals. Still the process remained civil until national events in May, 1970, changed everything: on April 30th, President Nixon announced that United States forces had joined the South Vietnamese army in the invasion of Cambodia, where North Vietnam had established an out-of-reach sanctuary for the Viet Cong and the North Vietnam regular army which had joined the fight. Immediately the nation, feeling betrayed by a president who had been elected to end the war instead of expanding it, exploded in protest. On college campuses, a number of ROTC facilities were fire-bombed; then, on May 4, National Guard troops at Kent State University, called to keep order, responded to provocations with shots that killed four students and wounded nine. This event galvanized students everywhere, including Valparaiso, into action. On Tuesday, May 5, student leaders called for a complete shut-down of the university. While more than 2000 students and faculty participated in a march to the downtown court house, by Wednesday support for the shut-down was waning. When President Huegli maintained that the proper course of action was to return to classes and that a day of mourning would be held on Friday, the student leaders reacted negatively.

College administration buildings across the nation were under siege. The focus at Valparaiso was on Kinsey Hall which, in addition to housing the music department, was the location of President Huegli's office. Late in the evening it was reported that students were marching to Kinsey Hall with the intention of occupying the president's office. In the early hours of the next morning, Kinsey Hall was on fire. By the time the fire was put out, the building had been completely destroyed. Three students, who were never publicly identified by the administration as the arsonists, were quietly expelled without being charged for the crime.

Valparaiso University began the decade of the 1970s damaged both emotionally and financially. Despite the best efforts of students and administration, the school did suffer from the violent excesses of May,

1970, and its recovery was complicated by several factors. On a philosophical level, the faculty and administration needed to adjust to the loss of absolute control of the curriculum and student residential life. More practically, new facilities for the music program were immediately required, making the poor financial condition of the university even worse. In order to recover from a severe budget deficit in 1969-70, tuition was raised by 21% in spite of great concern that this would price Valparaiso out of its market. Certainly the tuition increase was one of the factors in the enrollment decline of the early 70s. President Huegli worked hard and with good effect to put the University back on solid footing in spite of a difficult external environment.

Two additional factors contributed to the difficulties as well. The decade began with unrest in the Lutheran Church-Missouri Synod whose members were the primary source of students and financial support. Newly elected in 1969, the conservative president and board members of the synod brought charges of teaching false doctrine against the president and some faculty of the seminary. Those charged left to form a "seminary in exile" in 1974. In the minds of the more conservative synod pastors and members, Valparaiso was identified with the liberal faction of the synod and the exiled seminary. Many withdrew their financial support and discouraged Lutheran students from attending Valparaiso. Also complicating the financial stability of the university was the OPEC oil embargo of 1973, which ushered in a period of high inflation. The Consumer Price Index increased by 112% during the decade. Not too surprisingly, these factors resulted in a decline in the undergraduate enrollment from a high of 3859 in 1969 to 3166 in 1976, before recovering to 3372 in 1979. Faculty and staff salaries, not great to begin with, failed to keep pace with the cost of living.

Despite operating funds being very tight, Valparaiso was able to find donors for capital improvements. A gift from Alfred and Elfrieda LeBien was used to construct LeBien Hall for the College of Nursing in 1970. Dickmeyer Hall was completed in 1972 using insurance proceeds from the Kinsey Hall fire. The Klingsick Addition to Neils was completed in 1973 and the physics laboratories were moved from Baldwin Hall. Also in 1973 Commercial/Engineering/Benton Hall, almost 100 years old, was finally razed. A grant from the Lutheran Spencer Werner Foundation enabled the construction of the law library addition to Wesemann Hall in 1976. A gift from the Urschel family and a grant from the Krannert Foundation were used to construct Urschel Hall for the College of Business Administration in 1979.

In 1974 President Huegli announced to the faculty that the deficit had been removed and that a fund drive, "Forward to the Eighties" had been initiated with a goal of $28.15 million, of which $10 million was for endowment. In 1978, at the end of his presidency, President Huegli was able to report that the $700,000 deficit had been replaced with an operating reserve of $2.7 million and the endowment had been increased from $1.7 to $15.7 million. The university was again in a stable financial condition.

THE COLLEGE OF ENGINEERING IN THE 1970S

By and large, the engineering faculty and students were not actively involved in the campus protests. In many small ways engineering students did question the status quo, but there was no significant organized agitation. In fact, their lack of active support during the Kent

Early Digital Computer

State protests so angered student protest leaders that vague threats were made to target Gellersen Hall for attack. Engineering students did show solidarity with their Arts and Sciences classmates in their dress and grooming, however. Some faculty had great difficulty dealing with bare feet, beards, and long hair in the classroom and they aggressively enforced what they believed to be professional standards. But with time things did quiet down.

The college of engineering began the decade with Dean Kruger leading a faculty of 19. Of those, eight had earned the Ph.D. degree. After serving as dean for 8 years, Kruger chose to return to the faculty full-time at the start of the 1972-73 academic year. Professor Gilbert Lehmann of the mechanical engineering faculty was appointed acting dean while the college conducted a search for a permanent replacement. The search resulted in Lehmann's appointment in January, 1973. Department chairmen at the start of the decade were Charles Peller, civil engineering; William Shewan, electrical engineering; and Leslie Zoss, mechanical engineering.

Dean Lehmann did not pick the best time to take over the leadership of the College. As with the university at large, the solid enrollments of the expansion-minded 1960s had given way to a steep decline in new students. From 1970 to 1972, freshman engineering enrollment dropped from 144 to 122 to 82. Political activism and distaste for anything related to defense and the Cold War had made the study of engineering very unpopular to high school students during the late 1960s. Nationally, freshman engineering enrollments dropped from about 80,000 in 1966 to about 52,000 in 1973, even though the total number of "baby boom" 18-year-olds continued to increase. Adding to the enrollment problem for private universities was the proliferation of new engineering programs at the expanding second-tier state universities. From 1962 to 1973, the number of institutions with accredited engineering programs increased from 162 to 225. Regaining student enrollment became the primary order of business for Dean Lehmann and the college. In a move to advertise the college and promote enrollment, Professor Zoss created and promoted summer and weekend programs for high school students, the first one being called Potential Engineers Week or PEW. In time it was renamed Future Engineers Week. Faculty also began a program of calling prospective students to encourage their enrollment. Fortunately, either these initiatives worked or the down cycle ended itself naturally. By 1976 the college had a freshman class of 159, the largest in its history and freshman enrollment topped out at 166 in 1978.

In earlier years, college administrators had hoped to add a Master's degree program as well as additional undergraduate majors. Now, though, a combination of several factors quietly ended such discussions. The college had been battered by general campus unrest and erratic enrollment. There was little national acceptance of the ASEE Goals of Engineering Education recommendation to make the Master's degree the first professional degree, and the college was continually under financial stress.

In spite of the financial constraints of the decade, the academic credentials of the faculty continued to strengthen. The decade began with engineering faculty salaries 20-25% below those at comparable schools. A self-study prepared for the ECPD visit in 1978 documented that the average assistant professor salary in the college was slightly less than the average starting pay of new mechanical engineering graduates.

GILBERT MARK LEHMANN

Gilbert Lehmann was born on August 6, 1933, in Libertyville, Illinois. After graduating from Libertyville High School in 1951, he enrolled in the College of Engineering at Valparaiso, and was awarded a B.S.M.E. in 1955. After a year of graduate study at the Illinois Institute of Technology, he joined the faculty at Valparaiso as an instructor in civil engineering. While teaching at Valparaiso, he completed his work at IIT and earned the M.S.M.E. in 1957. He was then appointed to the mechanical engineering faculty. From 1961 to 1966 he took a leave to complete his doctorate at Purdue University's rocket lab in the mechanical engineering department. He was awarded the Ph.D. in 1966. From 1972 to 1978 he served as dean of the college. After concluding his service as dean, he continued to teach thermodynamics courses in the mechanical engineering program until his retirement in 1995. His daughter, Susan, taught for one year in the civil engineering department and his brother Joel has been a long-time member of the mathematics and computer science faculty.

Under ECPD prodding, a significant improvement was made the next year; but even without competitive salaries, at the start of the 1979-80 year 14 of the 22 faculty held the Ph. D. degree. Among those faculty added during this period, six made teaching at Valparaiso their career: Robert Rose in 1969, William Schoech and Daniel Hart, in 1970, Bradford Spring in 1971, Michael Doria in 1976, and John Steffen in 1977. During the decade, the chairmanship of each of the departments changed. Edgar Luecke succeeded William Shewan in 1973, William Schoech replaced Leslie Zoss in 1977, and Bradford Spring took over from Charles Peller in 1978. In 1974, two years after he had returned to the teaching faculty, Fred Kruger accepted the position of Vice President for Business Affairs, holding it until he retired in 1989. In university life, President Albert Huegli, who had reached the mandatory retirement age, was succeeded by Robert Schnabel in 1978.

Having weathered the difficult times of the early 1970s and with the college again on the upswing, Dean Lehmann was granted a sabbatical leave for the 1978-79 year, during which William Shewan served as acting dean. When during his sabbatical year Dean Lehmann decided to return to teaching, Shewan continued for a second year as acting dean. During that second year, the faculty requested that only candidates from off-campus be considered to replace Dean Lehmann.

DIGITAL COMPUTERS

The decade of the 1970s marked the real start of the academic use of digital computers at Valparaiso. The catalog of 1967-68 noted that an academic computer center would be installed in Gellersen Center when it opened in January, 1968. The IBM 1620 that had been located on the west campus was moved into a specially designed space in Gellersen. In 1969 the IBM 1620 was replaced by a used IBM 1710, which was an upgraded IBM 1620 with A/D and D/A capabilities. When it was installed at Valparaiso it was at least one generation old, since it had been withdrawn from the market in 1965. Aware that this was not a leading-edge computer, a faculty committee recommended upgrading the computer resources; however, the difficult financial condition of the early 1970s prevented any purchases.

The computer center in Gellersen followed the paradigm of larger computer centers with a staff that interfaced between the user and the computer. By the early 1970s various scientific electronic calculators, including some that were programmable, were on the market. To bring the computer user closer to the computer, Dean Kruger led the development of a special lab that contained several of these rudimentary computers for student use. This lab was an important bridge to more modern computing. In spite of opposition from some faculty traditionalists, in 1973 new students were no longer required to own and use a quality slide rule. The era of Dean Hesse's precision 20-inch slide rule was officially over.

Concerned that Valparaiso was falling far behind, another faculty committee convinced the administration that it had to act. Professor John Sorensen, director of the academic computer center, developed a plan to replace the batch-process, punched-card-input IBM 1710 with a Hewlett Packard 3000 II, a time-share machine first introduced by HP in 1973. Financial resources were found, a classroom in Gellersen was appropriated as a computer terminal room, and the machine was installed in 1977. The college of engineering's programmable computer lab was then closed.

Curriculum Development

The most significant curriculum development in this period was the full implementation of required senior research project courses. The mechanical program had instituted a project course in the early 1960s. The other two departments had offered a "Senior Problem" course as an elective for selected students until 1969 when the civil program required a senior course similar to the one in mechanical engineering. Finally, after the EE department instituted a one-semester required course in 1972, the entire senior project requirement was regularized with identical course descriptions. This model remained in essentially the same format until 2000.

A problem that has puzzled engineering educators almost from the beginning is how to orient new students to the study of engineering. The

Mann Report of 1918 expressed the need for some kind of orientation course for freshmen as one way to counter the excessive failure rate. While it determined that the primary reason for failure was the poor academic preparation of incoming students, it also cited their lack of understanding of what it meant to be an engineer. Over time a fairly standard response to this problem has been a freshman engineering orientation lecture course. At Valparaiso a non-credit freshman "Engineering Lectures" course was instituted in 1947. Responding to the fact that students did not appreciate the orientation lectures (students often re-titled them "Sleep 100"), this course was changed in the mid-1950s to instruction in engineering calculations using the slide rule, but augmented with a few professional orientation lectures.

Attempts at orientation were eliminated in 1960 but resurrected in 1968 in a new form as a one credit engineering laboratory for freshmen, a format which lasted for just three years. It was replaced by a two-credit engineering calculation course which included orientation lectures about the three engineering majors. With the development of the engineering computer lab, computation using programmable electronic calculators began to replace slide rule techniques. By 1975 this course had been split again into two courses without any orientation lectures, the first semester concentrating on computation and the second introducing programming in the FORTRAN computer language. The growing importance of computer programming and the installation of the HP 3000 precipitated

WILLIAM SHEWAN
The academic career path of William "Bill" Shewan was anything but usual. He was born on May 24, 1914, in Chicago, but when he was a youth, his family relocated to a small farm outside Valparaiso, a farm that he continued to work for many years while he taught at the university. He attended Valparaiso High School for two years, until at the age of 16, in 1930, he went to work to help support his parents. He developed an interest in radio electronics and, enlisting in the Navy at the start of World War II, was accepted into its training course for radio technicians. He and a Valparaiso friend who had studied radio theory with him achieved the top two scores in the nation on the qualification exam for this course. After service in the Pacific until the end of the war, he worked for a short time for the local electrical utility and earned his GED high school diploma in 1946. In 1947 he enrolled at

another change in 1979. A three-credit "Introduction to Algorithms for Computing" was required in the first semester and a three-credit "Engineering Laboratory," stressing lab techniques and report writing, in the second semester. For the most part, this addition made up for the loss of laboratory experience when the standard physics course taught by the physics department was eliminated in the 1960s. However, this lab course was very difficult to staff and manage; it was eliminated in 1983.

As can be seen from changes in the freshman program during the 1970s, how to respond to the emergence of digital computers was a continuing challenge for curriculum designers. A decision had been made in the mid-1960s that the mathematics department would take the lead in digital computer instruction, along with responsibility for operating an instructional computer. In 1966 the College of Engineering began requiring instruction in the fundamentals of both analog and digital computers. Since the speed and capacity of digital computers, except on the largest mainframes at the premier research facilities, were insufficient to tackle anything but the simplest differential equations, analog computers were considered far superior for their solution. But by 1975, the performance of digital computers had improved so much that instruction in analog computers was eliminated and the analog computer lab disbanded. In that same year, as engineering freshmen were introduced to digital computers and the FORTRAN language, each department began to consider how to integrate digital computer

---

Valparaiso University as an applied science major in the physics department and began teaching electronics at Valparaiso Technical Institute, the successor of the Dodge telegraphy school. He received the Bachelor's degree in 1950 and began teaching in the College of Engineering in 1951.

While teaching, farming, and starting a family, Dr. Shewan commuted to Notre Dame where he earned an M.S.E.E. in 1952. He continued graduate work at Purdue by commuting to West Lafayette and earned the Ph.D. in 1966. His special teaching and research interests were in automatic control theory and electromagnetic field theory. By 1955 he was the senior faculty member in the electrical engineering department and was instrumental in guiding the development of the college in those early years. He served as head and then chair of the department until 1973 and as acting dean of the college from 1978 to 1980. Bill retired at age 70 in 1984, enjoying an active retirement until his death on January 11, 2006.

programming and applications into its curriculum. By 1981 each had sorted out its approach: the CE department required nothing beyond the introductory course, the ME department required a second course emphasizing numerical methods for mechanical engineering problems, and the EE curriculum moved toward courses in the engineering of computers. All students who wanted more programming were able to take electives in the newly established computer science major.

CURRICULUM CHANGES IN THE DEPARTMENTS

In addition to curriculum changes applicable to all engineers, including increasing credits from 136 to 138 and reducing the common core to three semesters, each department made adjustments in its offerings. The explosive growth in the importance of digital technology required significant adjustments to the electrical engineering curriculum, but had little effect on the core offerings in mechanical and civil engineering. In civil engineering work in soil mechanics and water resources was strengthened, courses in engineering management and statistics were added, and the second course in electrical engineering was eliminated. In mechanical engineering the core courses were essentially unchanged. The

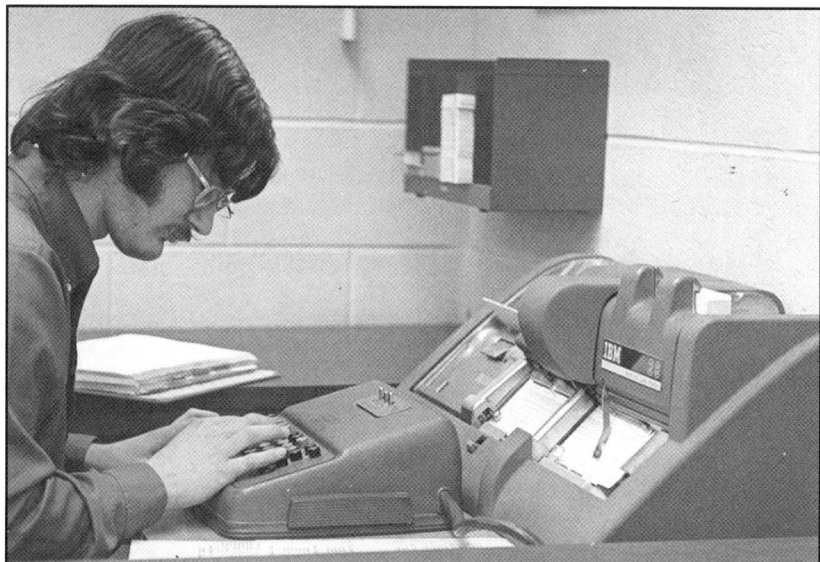

The Dreaded Key Punch for IBM Cards

second course in machine design became an elective; three elective courses in thermodynamic applications were repackaged into a single heat power design course; and a second drawing course that included some computer-aided drawing was added. Production operations, numerical control of tool systems, and a topics course were added to the existing experimental stress analysis, automatic control, and vibrations electives.

The electrical engineering courses were considerably reorganized to respond to the increasing importance of digital applications. The optional course in digital design, which had been absorbed into the electronics course, was replaced with an optional course in microprocessor applications. In 1979 a computer organization course was required of all EE students. Discrete-time system theory was added to the system theory sequence. Half-semester elective courses in power electronics, communication electronics, and selected topics plus a full semester elective in power systems engineering were added to the existing electives in microwave electronics and servomechanism design.

Under the direction of Professor Rodney Bohlmann, a microcomputer lab was created. A 1970 graduate of Valparaiso, he completed a Ph.D. in computer engineering at Rice University in 1974, and joined the VU faculty in 1975 after two years of teaching at the University of Texas at Austin. In 1979 the lab contained two SWTP microcomputers, 12 Motorola 6800 development systems, and an Altair 8800 microcomputer. Using his experience with the SWTP microcomputers and a grant from the Valparaiso Guild, he led the college in establishing a faculty word processing and spread sheet facility using the SWTP system in 1982. This was the first such system on the campus for either faculty or student use. It was not long before others followed. Those interested in the history of computers will remember that the Altair 8800 was the computer kit for which Bill Gates and Paul Allen wrote the original DOS operating system that became the genesis of the Microsoft Corporation.

Although two separate degree programs became available in 1984, both still relied on a core of linear circuits, electronics, linear system theory, and digital design courses. The computer engineering program replaced field theory, analog design, energy conversion, and computer organization with four courses from the computer science major. Elective courses for the two programs were communication theory, communication electronics, microwaves, microprocessors, computer networks, power systems, servomechanisms, power electronics, and computer system architecture.

The IBM 1710 – Professor Isbel on the left and Instructor Kusch on the right. In the center, unknown.

THE EARLY 1980S

After a relatively stable period in the 1970s, changes were on the way for the college of engineering. Two external events at the turn of the decade contributed significantly to these changes. First, the United States began 1980 by entering the worst recession in 50 years, its cause being the monetary actions taken to stop the runaway inflation of the previous decade. The recession tightened the job market for engineers and had the usual effect of reducing freshman engineering enrollment. Second, and more lasting, was the arrival of personal computers. In the late 1970s, a variety of personal computers appeared on the market, although all except Apple are now just a memory. The 8088 microprocessor, introduced in 1979 by Intel, was used for the design of the first IBM PC, introduced in 1981. By using the non-proprietary operating system supplied by Microsoft, it opened the way for standardization and commoditization of personal computers. The entry of IBM into the market was a sure signal that personal computers were important, and their impact on curriculum was felt almost immediately.

The 1980-81 year began with the installation of James Scroggin as dean. He came to Valparaiso from the University of Wisconsin at Platteville where he had served as chairman of the mechanical engineering department. Just a few weeks into the semester, the college was shocked by the sudden and unexpected death of Professor Peller of the civil engineering department. As a WWII veteran and graduate student at Illinois Institute of Technology, he had come to Valparaiso along with Dean Hesse in 1949. Two other long-time professors ended their service in 1983. Dr. William Shewan reached the mandatory retirement age. Dr. Leslie Zoss was granted a leave to become the president of the Instrument Society of America, the primary professional organization for those working in the process control industry. During his leave he chose to establish a full-time consultancy to that industry.

The two most significant initiatives of the college during the early 80s were the establishment of the co-operative education program and the addition of a computer engineering degree program. The co-op program was created entirely through the effort and perseverance of Dean Scroggin. His experience at the University of Cincinnati, where the first engineering co-op education programs were developed some 60 years earlier, made him an ideal person to introduce this style of education to Valparaiso. At a time of tight employment conditions, co-op employment historically has given students an advantage in finding good employment after graduating. The time was right for Valparaiso to start a co-op program. In addition to obtaining a generous grant from the federal government to finance the start-up costs for the program, he also guided the entire process of winning acceptance for a proposal that academic credit be awarded for the experience during the work period. Student performance at the work site was monitored by faculty visits, and written reports were required at the end of each work assignment. The program was first offered in 1983-84. To handle promotion of the program and administrative details, he recruited Professor Norman Jensen, a retired Air Force Colonel with ROTC administrative experience who had joined the mechanical engineering faculty in 1981. Professor Jensen enthusiastically promoted and shepherded the program, finding industrial partners and assuring that the work assignments merited academic credit. From 10 co-op students when the program started in 1983 the program grew quickly to 57 in 1989. These 57 constituted 47% of the students who met the minimum eligibility criterion of a 2.4 GPA.

In 1981 the mathematics department initiated a computer science major that was available to new freshmen and renamed itself the mathematics and computer science department. Nationally, the teaching of computer science resided primarily in mathematics or electrical engineering departments. At a number of engineering schools, the EE departments were adapting parts of computer science and parts of electrical engineering into a new computer engineering degree. Strong interest in computer courses among EE students at Valparaiso and the introduction of the full computer science major encouraged the college to consider how it could offer a computer engineering degree as a complement to the computer science major. Since this would require cooperation between colleges, administratively it would not be as clean as if it were happening within one college. A computer engineering committee composed of three electrical engineering and three computer science faculty members was established to plan and supervise the curriculum for a new degree program. Following the recommendation of the national leaders in the movement to create this new engineering degree, the degree was called "Bachelor of Science in Computer Science and Engineering." Beginning with 1984-85 year, the EE department changed

JAMES T. SCROGGIN
Born in Covington, Kentucky on September 18, 1931, James Scroggin graduated from Romulus High School in Romulus, Michigan in 1949. From 1951 to 1954 he attended the Detroit Bible College, after which he joined the Ford Motor Company as a trainee in chassis layout and design. In 1958 he enrolled at the Indiana Institute of Technology where he earned a B.S.M.E. in 1960. After earning an M.S.M.E. at Michigan State University in 1962, he became an instructor at the University of Cincinnati while continuing graduate work. In 1968 he earned the Ph.D. at Cincinnati, specializing in mechanical design. After serving for seven years on the engineering faculty of Ohio Northern University, he took the position

its name to the electrical and computer engineering department, and the new degree was made available to current students who could arrange their course work to meet the degree requirements. Eight graduates were awarded the new degree in 1986. Finding that the degree name caused confusion among both students and employers, the name of the degree was changed to "Computer Engineering" after the first class graduated.

The Academic Computer Center Moves to Schnabel Hall

At the outset academic computer usage was concentrated in engineering, mathematics, and the sciences. As usage grew after the installation of the HP 3000, it became apparent that space in Gellersen was not adequate to serve the demand. In 1980s technology it was still necessary that the time-share terminals be physically near the computer. Access through telephone modems was available but the campus was not effectively wired for remote access. Planning for a new building to house the computer, computer classrooms, and office for support personnel was begun in 1983. During the same time, a significant upgrade was being planned for what was still called the journalism department, its main feature being a TV studio for broadcast journalism. Plans for these two needs were combined, and one building with the required space and environmental controls for electronic equipment was designed. The Academic Computer and Communications Building, now called Schnabel Hall, was completed in September, 1984. The College of

---

of Chair of Industrial and Mechanical Engineering at the University of Wisconsin – Platteville. In 1980 he was appointed Dean of Engineering at Valparaiso and served until 1985.

Using his experiences with co-operative education at the University of Cincinnati, Dean Scroggin obtained federal government grants to start co-op programs, first in the College of Engineering and then in the College of Business Administration. Co-op programs are now firmly established throughout the university. After leaving Valparaiso, he served as dean of engineering at the University of Bridgeport until 1989 and then as chair of the department of engineering at Messiah College, Grantham, Pennsylvania, until he retired in 1997.

Engineering took over the vacated space in Gellersen for faculty and staff offices.

ENROLLMENT TRENDS

Enrollment in the college rose rapidly in the late 1970s, from a low of 334 in 1974 to 516 in 1980. In 1981, it peaked at 534 and remained above 500 until 1985. The number of graduates peaked in 1985 at 117, corresponding exactly with the national peak of approximately 78,000 graduates in the same year. Nationally this number was 85% greater than 1977; at Valparaiso the increase during the same period was 67%. Enrollment in computer science also reached its peak in the same year, was flat until 1987, and then began to decline in 1988. Interestingly, the 1985 peak corresponded with a minimum in the social sciences and psychology and was just a few years earlier than the minimum in the biological sciences. At Valparaiso, the increases occurred in the electrical and mechanical degrees. Civil degrees slowly declined, bottoming out in 1990.

Throughout the 1960s a few women had enrolled in engineering at Valparaiso but until the start of the next decade none persisted to earn a

Analog Computer – Professor Shewan and Students

degree. This circumstance was not too unusual considering that, of the approximately 45,000 engineering degrees awarded nationally in 1970, women earned only 358. From 1970 to 1976 at Valparaiso only one woman each year earned a degree. Then, for the final four years of the decade, women graduates averaged about 10% of the class. From this group of women, 1978 graduates Linda Ivett Allen and Lorraine Gaunt Dorrough have volunteered their services to the university, Allen as member of its National Council and Dorrough as the national president of the Valparaiso Guild. By 1985, 15 women graduates and 10 international graduates added a welcome diversity to the 117 students awarded degrees that year. There were enough women engineers to found a student section of the Society of Women Engineers in 1987. The Society has become an integral part of the academic and social life of the college.

Faculty Additions

Enrollment grew rapidly during the early 1980s. Among the 18 who received faculty appointments, the following remained at Valparaiso for the remainder of their teaching careers: Norman Jensen and Demos Gelopulos in 1981, Gerald Seeley in 1983, and Daniel Goodman in 1985. L. Alan Kraft, who also joined the faculty in 1985, remains an active faculty member.

Developments in Engineering Education

Throughout the 1970s and early 1980s the number of colleges offering engineering and engineering technology continued to increase. In 1985, 263 schools offered engineering courses, an increase of 38% from 1968. In the same period, the number of accredited engineering degree programs rose to 1336, an increase of 41%. The growth of the number of schools offering engineering technology programs was even more impressive. These increased by 330% to 207 in 1985. The number of individual engineering technology degree programs increased by 365% to 739 during the period. Many of these new programs were established at branch campuses of state universities and at state normal schools that were rapidly being converted to general universities.

Since it was essentially a volunteer organization, ECPD found it difficult to adequately manage its accreditation activities as the number of visits increased, even though it lengthened the period of accreditation to six years. Not only had the number of site visits increased, but finding and training professionals to make the accreditation visits became even more difficult. The time commitment alone was demanding: an accreditation visitor can expect to volunteer the equivalent of one work-week in preparing, visiting, and reporting. ECPD had been created by engineering faculty through their ASEE professional organization, and faculty were still, by and large, willing to take the time for this professional service. However, one clear criticism from the professional engineering societies was that faculty did not adequately or fairly represent the profession at large. To answer this criticism, ECPD began to recruit enough engineers from professional practice so that faculty comprised only half the visit team. Within a short time complaints came in from the programs visited that these non-educators, whose own engineering education may have been 20 or 30 years ago, did not fully understand the current engineering education system and, even worse, were applying their own criteria instead of the published criteria.

A second problem with accreditation, not related to the growth of the number of programs, was the growing expectation from all facets of society for due process. Until 1965, ECPD's accreditation decisions were impossible to challenge. In that year the Engineering Technology Accreditation Commission of ECPD offered schools the opportunity to review and correct perceived errors of fact or interpretation before the final decision was made. Following this lead, the Engineering Accreditation Commission extended due process to engineering programs in 1973.

One unanticipated outcome of adding due process and practicing engineers to the accreditation process was the huge increase in the number of accreditation criteria. Criteria are divided into two parts: general and degree specific. Before the late 50s the general criteria required only one column of type; until 1970 only two columns were needed. By 1985 the number was 15 columns! At the same time, each professional engineering society was developing its own guidelines, and visitors often used them instead of the official ECPD criteria. In 1982 a process was completed to incorporate these guidelines into official criteria. When this happened, virtually the complete engineering curriculum was specified and critics complained that possibilities for creative curriculum innovations would be lost and that accreditation had become nothing but "bean counting." By the early 1990s a new paradigm for accreditation called "Engineering Criteria 2000" was being developed.

In 1980 ECPD became ABET, the Accreditation Board for Engineering and Technology. For years leaders in the various engineering professional societies had been trying to develop an organization that could speak for the entire engineering profession on issues beyond the scope of the ECPD charter. Their solution was to form the American Association of Engineering Societies in 1980. This new association assumed responsibility for the old ECPD areas of professional development, ethics, and guidance, leaving accrediting as the only activity for the new ABET. ABET created an Engineering Accreditation Commission and a Technology Accreditation Commission and gave each full authority to accredit. The ABET board acted only on appeals of "not to accredit" decisions. Because it was well respected for the quality of its accreditation process, other professional societies, not strictly engineering or technology, came to ABET with requests that it handle their accreditation process. When in 1983, ABET created a third commission, the Related Accreditation Commission, the computer science profession was one of the first to request ABET to manage its accreditation process.

NINE

RESPONDING TO CHANGE: 1985-2009

Only a very keen observer in 1985 could have predicted the state of engineering education, Valparaiso University, and the College of Engineering in the year 2000. The coming end of the Cold War and a wide-spread concern for American industrial competitiveness ushered in not only a shift in the orientation of engineering curricula from science/national defense to design/industrial practice but also a radical reorientation of accreditation criteria. At Valparaiso this shift resulted in revisions of the common core curriculum and the senior project course as well as the development of formal program assessment procedures.

The improvement in performance and the decrease in cost of digital computers caused the development of new and better engineering application programs and a steady shift to computing with personal computers. As new applications became available and entering students became increasingly sophisticated in computer use, the college undertook an almost yearly rethinking of curricula and course content. The college was not able to maintain continuing accreditation of the computer engineering program until the new ABET criteria became effective.

At the university level, the financial pressures that accompanied rising aspirations required greater involvement of college faculty and staff in student recruitment and fund-raising. For the first time since the Venture of Faith, the College of Engineering was included as a component in two general fund-raising campaigns: Three Goals – One Promise in the late 1990s and Our Valpo – Our Time, which concluded in 2009. In a definite break from previous efforts, college leaders were actively involved in both campaigns.

CHANGES IN ENGINEERING EDUCATION

The shape of engineering education is heavily influenced by accreditation standards and criteria. By the late 1980s, leading engineering educators were becoming convinced that ABET accreditation was standing in the way of the kinds of innovations required to keep pace with the changing environment for engineering practice. Since the 1950s education priorities had been dominated by the national needs created by the Cold War and the Space Race. At the height of President Reagan's "Star Wars" defense initiative in 1985, the deteriorating condition of the Soviet Union's economy led to the elevation of Mikhail Gorbachev to its leadership. His reform policies failed to stop the economic decline, the Berlin Wall fell in 1989, and the Soviet Union ceased to exist in 1991. Both the Cold War and the Space Race were over. As the military threat of the Soviet Union declined, the United States had growing concerns that, while it had been building a military superiority which the Soviets could not match, it had ceded commercial and consumer production to Japan. Wide-spread concern about the competitiveness of American manufacturing industries began to emerge.

Changes at ECPD/ABET

The effort in the 1970s of ECPD/ABET to promote greater involvement of practicing engineers in the accreditation process had an unexpected effect. Under the prodding of the professional engineering societies, ABET began to establish detailed specifications in curriculum goals and content that almost completely defined the education of an engineer. The science orientation that was developed in response to World War II had produced a generation of engineering graduates with fine technical skills well-fitted to the defense needs of the nation, but not so well suited to the needs of the non-defense industries. Part of the "criteria creep" causing significant trouble was the insistence of practicing professionals that educators were including too much engineering science and not enough engineering design in the curriculum. Educators were becoming increasingly frustrated with rigid demands that programs demonstrate the minimum one-half year of design. In many programs the pedagogy seamlessly mixed analysis and design in the same course so that it was often a matter of interpretation as to whether the minimums had been met. Leading engineering schools were receiving less than maximum terms of accreditation because of their failure to fulfill just one of the growing lists of criteria. The perceived need of state supported schools to maintain accreditation to satisfy their state legislatures constrained them in their desire to innovate and adapt to the new environments.

By 1992 a group of deans from leading schools was threatening to set up a rival accrediting agency if the situation did not change. This was a clear signal to ABET that it had to change its ways or cease to exist as a factor in engineering education. One immediate result was the merging of the engineering science and design categories into an engineering topics category that would not require detailed demonstration of design work. At the ABET annual meeting in 1992, the second outcome was that an Accreditation Process Review Committee was established to consider revision of the entire accreditation process. Out of this effort, in 1995 the first draft version of Engineering Criteria 2000 (EC2000) was distributed for comment from all stakeholders, with full implementation to begin in 2000. EC2000 essentially turns the evaluation process around: instead of numerical measures of inputs, it requires both measurement of outputs and a process to use assessment of these outputs to make continuous improvements. Each program is expected to set its goals and objectives in relationship to fourteen different areas of knowledge or abilities, with no numerical credit-hour goals set for any of them. A few programs were evaluated in 1998 and 1999 to test the process. Valparaiso was accredited under the guidelines of EC2000 in 2004, which was the scheduled time for the next review.

Changes at Valparaiso

At Valparaiso in 1985, Robert Schnabel was nearing the end of his tenure as President. A successful $50 million major fund-raising campaign, The Crusade for Valparaiso University, had resulted in a new building for the School of Law, the basketball arena addition to the athletics facilities, and the Communications and Computer Center which was later named in honor of President Schnabel. The campaign was so successful that it was extended and the goal was raised by another $22 million. When the Lutheran Church-Missouri Synod started a competing deaconess program, the Valparaiso program was reorganized and Deaconess Hall, a residence hall which had been owned by the independent Lutheran Deaconess Association, was purchased by the University, converted into faculty offices, and renamed Huegli Hall. Arts and Sciences faculty offices that had been housed in crumbling Lembke Hall were finally moved to the center of the campus. Also, after 40 years the dream of having an administration building was achieved. When the law school moved to its new building on the old campus, it took the Wesemann Hall building name with it. Administrative offices that had been scattered all over the campus were brought together to the original Wesemann Hall, an addition was added to house offices for the president and the vice-president for academic affairs, and the building renamed Kretzmann Hall. As a sign that Valparaiso University had finally become a viable enterprise, President Schnabel, as one of his last official acts in 1988, presided over the merger of the two legal entities that had run the university since the Lutheran purchase in 1925. Because of the complex financial situation of the Brown family, from whom the university real estate had been purchased, one corporation had been created to own the real estate and a second to operate the university. Now there was only the Lutheran University Association, doing business as Valparaiso University, and those faculty and staff who were not directly involved in business affairs no longer needed to be puzzled about which entity did what. The 1988-89 academic year began with Dr. Alan Harre succeeding Robert Schnabel as President.

Changes at the College of Engineering

At the College of Engineering, the 1985-86 year began with the appointment of Stuart Walesh as Dean. He succeeded James Scroggin who was not reappointed to a second five-year term. Dean Scroggin chose not to remain on the faculty and accepted an appointment as Dean of Engineering at the University of Bridgeport in Connecticut. Dean Walesh returned to his alma mater after 13 years of professional civil engineering practice in Wisconsin. A 1963 Civil Engineering graduate, he had done graduate work at Johns Hopkins and earned the Ph.D. at the University of Wisconsin in 1969. He taught civil engineering at Valparaiso from 1969 to 1972. Drawing on his years of experience in working in a large engineering organization, he set about bringing a greater degree of organization to the day-to-day affairs of the college. Convinced that the future of the college lay in establishing a reputation for high quality, he began to put in place policies that expected the highest performance from both students and faculty. To remind students that the non-engineering component of their curriculum was important, separate 2.0 minimum grade-point averages were established for the general education component and for the mathematics, science, and general engineering component. Not all students responded well and academic probation and suspension rates went up. For the faculty, documentation of performance in the areas of teaching, scholarship, and service was required for consideration of merit increases in salary. He encouraged and prodded the faculty into greater scholarly production, particularly in the area of engineering education.

Computer Engineering Accreditation

One of the first major issues that Dean Walesh confronted concerned accrediting the computer engineering program. Requesting accreditation by ABET for a new degree program can be done only after at least one class has graduated. Even though the first class had graduated in 1986, the college decided that it would submit the computer engineering program at the time of the next scheduled accreditation review in 1989. In preparation for that review, a spirited debate arose in the ECE

Stuart G. Walesh
Stuart Walesh assumed the leadership of the College of Engineering as its dean in 1985. He was born on May 19, 1941, in Two Rivers, Wisconsin, and enrolled as a freshman engineer at Valparaiso in 1959. While at Valparaiso, he was the founding president of the new Tau Beta Pi chapter. After graduating with a degree in civil engineering in 1963 he continued his education at the Johns Hopkins University where he earned an M.S.C.E. in 1965. In 1967, while completing his graduate studies at the University of Wisconsin where he was awarded the Ph.D. in 1969, he joined the Valparaiso faculty. In 1970 he took a position with the Southwestern Regional Planning Commission and then in 1978 he joined Donahue and Associates, both in Waukesha, WI, specializing in water resource engineering. Dr. Walesh served

department concerning whether the program would satisfy ABET criteria. ABET had become concerned about the proliferation of weak programs both in computer engineering and computer science during the 1980s and had become more prescriptive and restrictive in its criteria. It was not clear that the college's program would satisfy the guidelines as they were developing. Despite the opinion of a knowledgeable consultant that the computer engineering committee (three engineering faculty and three computer science faculty) would not satisfy the required minimum faculty size for a computer engineering degree program, the ECE faculty, in a split vote, recommended going forward with a submission. Since accreditation issues affect the entire college, the recommendation was presented to the entire faculty. Professor Bohlmann, the lead computer engineering faculty member, convinced the dean and faculty that he could lead the effort to a successful outcome. Department chairman Demos Gelopulos, who did not support the effort, asked to be relieved of his appointment.

The outcome of the 1989, visit and review by ABET resulted in all programs, including computer engineering, being accredited for three years, with another on-site review required in the 1992-93 academic year. Short of a decision to "show cause" why a program should receive continued accreditation, this is the most restrictive action that ABET can take. This result was somewhat typical of what was happening nationally and causing so much displeasure with ABET. Usually, if deficiencies are deemed significant, a report on how the cited deficiencies

---

as dean from 1985 to 1993 and remained as a member of the civil engineering faculty until 1999 when he retired to establish a consulting practice.

Dr. Walesh is the author of *Urban Surface Water Management* (Wiley, 1989), *Engineering Your Future* (ASCE Press, 2000), *Flying Solo: How to Start an Individual Practitioner Consulting Business* (Hannah Publishing, 2000), and *Managing & Leading: 52 Lessons Learned for Engineers* (ASCE Press, 2004). He is the author or co-author of over 200 publications and presentations in the areas of engineering, education, and management. He has received a number of awards including the Distinguished Service Citation from the College of Engineering at the University of Wisconsin and Engineer of the Year Award from the Indiana Society of Professional Engineers. He is a Distinguished Member of ASCE and a Diplomate of the Academy of Water Resources Engineers.

have been corrected is required after three years. The weakness of the computer engineering program may have made a return visit necessary. The outcome of the subsequent 1992 review, officially announced in October, 1993, was that all but the computer engineering program received the maximum term of accreditation. For computer engineering, ABET was concerned about the degree of institutional commitment to the program. Information about five specific concerns, including faculty stability and program enrollment, was requested in preparation for an on-site visit in 1995.

Faced with declining enrollments and continued faculty instability, acting dean Edgar Luecke determined that there was little chance that a report and visit would result in a favorable outcome and the program was terminated for entering students in 1994. For a terminated program, ABET procedures maintain accreditation for those students already enrolled in the program. To maintain the core of the computer engineering degree program without the name, a revised electrical engineering degree program was created that allowed a student to choose either a traditional electrical emphasis or a computer emphasis. The sweeping liberalization of ABET criteria for all degree programs in 2000 made it possible to reinstate the separate computer engineering degree in 2002.

EDGAR JACOB LUECKE
Valparaiso University has been an integral part of the life of Edgar Luecke for 51 years — from 1951 when he enrolled as a freshman engineer, until 2002 when he retired from the university. He was born on October 6, 1933, in Cleveland, Ohio, where he lived until enrolling at Valparaiso. After graduating with a B.S.E.E. in 1955, he accepted an appointment as instructor in the college of engineering. At the same time he began graduate work at the University of Notre Dame, earning an M.S.E.E. there in 1957. From 1964 to 1966 he took a leave to complete residency requirements at Purdue University where he received his Ph.D. in 1968. His primary academic interests were in communication theory and electromagnetic field theory. For many years the college used his self-

Curriculum Revision

A second initiative during Dean Walesh's tenure was a major revision of the curriculum. In the 30 years since the curriculum had been revised to move instruction in basic physics from the physics department to the college of engineering, only a few changes were made in the curriculum. Most of them were internal to the electrical and computer engineering programs, as the department revised courses to accommodate the digital revolution. Except for accommodating computers, none changed the basic structure of the lower division curriculum. By 1990 a number of factors were coming together to cause the faculty to rethink the structure of the first year curriculum. After reaching a peak enrollment in 1985, both nationally and locally engineering enrollment was declining rather significantly. With lower numbers of entering freshmen and more aggressive expectations for their academic performance, the faculty was concerned with finding ways to increase the number of students who persisted into the sophomore year. The perception was that students wanted to begin work in their specific engineering major immediately, rather than going through three semesters of a common curriculum. In addition, the faculty felt that the three-semester delayed start on major courses made it difficult to reach, in only five semesters, the level of performance that employers expected of graduating seniors. Finally, with the development of software applications for engineering and the growing computer sophistication of entering freshmen, it was becoming

---

published text *Basic Electricity* for the electrical portion of its basic science courses. From 1973 to 1985 and again from 1988 to 1991 he served as chairman of the electrical and computer engineering department. From 1993 to 1999 he served first as acting dean and then dean of the college and then again from 2001 to 2002 as acting dean.

Throughout the years he served on many university-wide committees and task forces. As chairman of the campus planning and space allocation committee, he oversaw the creation of the current campus master plan. In 1987 the Valparaiso Alumni Association recognized him with its Distinguished Teaching Award; in 2003 he received its O. P. Kretzmann award for "Distinguished Contributions and Long Time Exemplary Service to Valparaiso University."

very difficult to craft an introductory computer course that met the needs of all programs and students.

The solution to these concerns was the introduction of a new curriculum at the start of the 1992-1993 year. The common-core of courses was reduced from three semesters to one and instruction in basic physics was returned to the physics department. To provide freshmen with some survival skills and information helpful in selecting a major as early as the second semester, a new "Exploring Engineering" course was introduced. A weekly recitation section introduced students to basic computer literacy, operating systems, and some software tools. For the first time in the history of engineering education at Valparaiso, engineering drawing, mechanics, basic electricity, and chemistry were not required of all students. Only mechanical engineers took a drawing course, called "Computer-Aided Design" rather than engineering graphics. All electrical and computer courses were dropped from the civil program and surveying was moved to the freshman year. Mechanics courses and chemistry became electives for electrical engineers and a third-semester structured computer language course replaced the first semester computer algorithms course. In the second semester the EEs took an introductory course in analog and digital circuits, and the computer engineers began with a digital design course. The mechanical department added a course in mechatronics and adapted its computer applications course to include instruction in computer languages. In the mood for change, each department made some additional changes in the upper-division curriculum. The number of credits required for the degree remained at 136 for several more years but was reduced to 132 in 1997 to bring the number in line with other engineering programs. By 1999 both the ECE and ME departments had made a further two-credit reduction.

While course titles remained the same, the pervasive impact of digital computing as an engineering tool was rapidly changing the content of virtually all courses. Even in non-digital courses, computer applications such as PSpice and Matlab revolutionized design and analysis techniques for electric and electronic systems. Finite-element analysis and solid modeling software revolutionized the teaching of machine design.

Manufacturing courses introduced computer-controlled machining processes. Spreadsheets allowed easy iteration of "what-if" approaches to design questions. For the faculty it was both an exciting and challenging time learning what to incorporate into courses and how to do it. In many cases that meant developing materials specific to the computer resources at Valparaiso.

The Return of Enrollment Challenges

In January, 1993, just as the new curriculum was getting off the ground, Dean Walesh announced that for personal reasons he would conclude his service as dean at the end of the academic year and return to the teaching faculty. While a search for a replacement was organized, Edgar Luecke was appointed to serve as acting dean for the next academic year. On the recommendation of the search committee he was appointed to a five-year term to start in 1994 and end in his 65th year in 1999. This start of his term coincided with another period of difficult finances for the university. Not only was engineering enrollment dropping, but the total number of new freshmen continued to slide alarmingly to a low of 553 for the fall semester of 1994. President Harre and the board of directors

Sun Workstation Laboratory-2009

concluded that drastic action was needed to bring operating expenses in line with operating income. With the assistance of a consultant, in December, 1994, President Harre announced a "transformation" plan that required extensive reductions in personnel. For the faculty, an attractive early-retirement plan was offered and accepted by 18. In all, 76 staff and faculty members were either retired or involuntarily terminated. The College of Engineering was required to reduce its faculty count by two, and that goal was met when two long-time members of the faculty, Merlyn Vocke and Gilbert Lehmann, chose early retirement.

It turned out that the enrollment decline for the university bottomed out in 1994. Nationally the low point in freshman engineering students occurred in 1995. Heightened competition for the declining pool of prospective students made enrollment management a primary focus for both Dean Luecke and the faculty. Faculty once again became more involved in the admissions process, as prospective students expected to interact with faculty during campus visits. Part of the enrollment decline in the mid-1990s was the result of a decrease in international students. Throughout the 1970s and early 1980s the college had a few international students, mostly from Middle Eastern countries and supported by their families. In the mid 1980s, having nationalized the Arabian American Oil Company (ARAMCO), the Saudi Arabian government began a program of developing a cadre of native Saudis to operate its facilities. Valparaiso was chosen as one of the American colleges to educate these students, with the Saudi government paying expenses. Later in the 1980s and early 1990s, Valparaiso benefited from a large influx of students from Malaysia. In its drive to modernize, the Malaysian government set up a program in which their engineering students would receive the first two years of engineering education in Malaysia in English with American faculty. When they had successfully completed this Indiana University-certified curriculum, they were supported by the government and placed at American engineering colleges. Professor Vocke spent the 1990-91 year teaching in this program in Malaysia. By 1994 Malaysia had established a local full four year engineering program and no new students enrolled at Valparaiso. The improving enrollment in the late 90s was partially due to the next group of government-sponsored students from the United Arab Emirates, another oil-rich nation also rapidly modernizing. Integrating Muslim students from other cultures who, in many cases, had more disposable money and much less practical experience than their American classmates was a challenge for the faculty.

Financial Campaigns

Financial campaigns are a staple of modern American higher education. The primary goal of the Lighting the Way campaign of the early 90s was the construction of the Center for the Arts, which was completed in 1997. This was an abbreviated campaign in preparation for a more extensive 1998 effort called Three Goals-One Promise, a $75 million campaign that included a component specifically for the College of Engineering. Dean Luecke and the faculty considered the most pressing needs for the college and established these priorities: endowed scholarships for engineering, improved resources to assist and mentor academically struggling students, physical improvements

Engineering Computational Laboratory - 2009

to 30-year-old Gellersen Center, an endowment to support orderly replacement of computer facilities, and staff to assist the college in program assessment requirements for ABET accreditation. The $9 million engineering goal consisted of $6 million for engineering scholarships, and $1 million each for a Learning Resource and Assessment Center (LRAC), the computer replacement endowment, and Gellersen building improvements. Two major gifts led the way. The Caterpillar Foundation provided a $2.5 million challenge gift to be allocated for scholarhips, faculty development, physical plant, and computer resources.   From the estate of Helen Hesse, the widow of Dean Herman Hesse, $3.6 million was received for engineering scholarships. Leadership gifts from engineering alumni were received from Donald Fites, Edward Tornberg, Richard Beumer, and Ralph Johnson. The AT&T Foundation provided $150,000 for the LRAC and the Leo Besozzi estate $500,000 for scholarships.

The primary capital goal of Three Goals – One Promise was a new building to replace Moellering Library, one of the first buildings on the new campus. It had become inadequate in size and could not suitably respond to the emergence of electronic information sources. In order to verify the best site for the new building, the existing campus plan was reviewed and a revised campus plan was developed, one which would encourage walking and discourage driving on campus. A ring-road plan was developed and a ceremonial entrance created from US 30. The south segment of this road was completed in 2006. The segment of Chapel Drive directly north of the Chapel was removed in 2007. The north segment of the ring road was completed in 2009. The Christopher Center for Library and Information Resources was dedicated in 2004. A second project of the campaign was an addition to Schnabel Hall to house the fast-growing meteorology program. The Kallay-Christopher Hall was dedicated in 2005.

Into the New Century

Dean Luecke concluded his term in 1999, returning to the faculty in a half-time capacity. After a national search, he was succeeded by Gerald

Seeley of the civil engineering department. Dean Seeley earned his undergraduate degree from the University of Wisconsin and his graduate degrees from the University of Minnesota. He joined the Valparaiso faculty in 1983 after serving as professor and dean at Tri-State (now Trine) University. For several years he had served as chair of the civil engineering department and was very active in broader university affairs. As Valparaiso University moved into the new century, active involvement in financial development for the college was added to the job description of the dean. The start of his term coincided with the transition from the silent to the public phase of the Three Goals – One Promise campaign and he enthusiastically met with friends and alumni throughout the country.

One of the first orders of business for Dean Seeley was initiating a new senior project course, in response to an ABET EC2000 accreditation criterion requiring graduates to function well on interdisciplinary teams. Each department considered how it could satisfy this new emphasis, and an interdisciplinary team senior design project seemed like the obvious avenue. When the senior project course had been established in the early 1970s, it was structured as a year-long senior independent thesis with an engineering science orientation. As the profession became more insistent in its demands to return more engineering design to the curriculum, the projects tended toward design rather than science. Some projects were organized around the work of two students, but all remained focused on a narrowly defined problem. Faculty initially considered creating teams made up of students from all four programs, but eventually decided that integrating a civil engineering component into every project was not feasible. The new courses were phased-in during the 1999-2000 year, with teams of 5 or 6 students for each project. For CE seniors, projects were developed to include all or most of the sub-disciplines of civil engineering, one student being responsible for each component of the project. The other two departments created projects that each had mechanical, electrical, and computer engineering components. Each project had an identifiable "customer," writing, speaking and project management components were emphasized to satisfy another EC2000 expected outcome.

During the second year of Dean Seeley's term, just as he was revealing his plans for a new Center of Entrepreneurship that would involve senior projects with an entrepreneur-in-residence, he was stricken with an unusual and fast-developing cancer. After an illness of just a few months, he died in April, 2001. The entire campus community was shocked by his death and paid its respects at a funeral service at the Chapel of the Resurrection.

With the end of the school year rapidly approaching, Professor Luecke was asked to put off his retirement and return to the dean's office to serve in an acting capacity until a new dean took office. During the vacancy he worked to carry on or complete projects started by Dean Seeley and to prepare the college for another search for a leader. The first completed project funded by the financial campaign was the construction and staffing of the Herman and Helen Hesse Learning Resource and Assessment Center, dedicated in October, 2001. One long-time component of the college's strategic plan was completed when the first Engineering National Council was recruited and held its first meeting in May, 2002. Office facilities were established for the first entrepreneur-in-residence who was developing a process for the environmentally important problem of treating hog-barn waste. While the idea had the potential for significant income for both the university and the entrepreneur, and had worked well in the prototype phase, it did not advance to commercialization. After further evaluation, other ways to introduce students to entrepreneurship were developed.

GERALD RAYMOND SEELEY
When Gerald "Jerry" Seeley was selected to be dean of the College of Engineering in 1999, it marked the second time that he had been a dean at an Indiana college. Prior to joining the Valparaiso faculty in 1983, he had served as dean of engineering at Tri-State (now Trine) University from 1978 to 1983. He was born October 9, 1940, in Wausau, Wisconsin. After a very brief career as a minor league baseball player in the Detroit Tigers organization, he started his academic career as an engineering student at Michigan Tech in 1958. A year later he transferred to the University of Wisconsin where he earned a B.S.M.E. in 1963. Then, after a year in industry at Union Carbide, the academic life called him back to earn an M.S. in Engineering Mechanics from Wisconsin in 1966. While

As part of his program to involve friends and alumni more closely in the support of the university, President Harre appointed an alumni advisory committee to work with the faculty in the search for the next dean. This committee, which included members of the board, was involved in drafting the position description, screening applicants, holding initial phone interviews, and conducting on-campus interviews. The search resulted in the appointment, in 2002, of alumnus Kraig Olejniczak, at that time on the faculty at the University of Arkansas. Dr. Olejniczak received his undergraduate degree in Electrical and Computer Engineering from Valparaiso in 1987 and M.S. and Ph.D. degrees from Purdue in 1988 and 1991.

Dean Olejniczak immediately began preparing the college for the ABET review to be conducted in 2004, the first for Valparaiso using the EC2000 criteria and procedures. Considerable effort in preparing documentation of assessment procedures and data helped toward a favorable outcome: accreditation of all programs, including computer engineering, for the maximum term. After some fine tuning, the revised senior project course produced a number of very interesting and well-crafted projects: many based on robotics were entered in national robotics competitions. Others responded to a university-wide emphasis on service learning by developing projects to provide sustainable irrigation in Kenya and wind power in Central America. The student designers spent part of their vacations traveling to the local villages selected for the installation of their project designs. Funded by a National Science Foundation grant,

---

working at Honeywell Corporation in Minneapolis he continued his graduate study at the University of Minnesota, earning an M.S.C.E. in 1971 and a Ph.D. specializing in structural engineering in 1973.

Dr. Seeley was very active in American Society for Engineering Education and was recognized with its Distinguished Service Award in 1997. He served as chairman of the civil engineering department from 1987 to 1991 and from 1998 to 1999. In 1998 he was named the first Paul and Cleo Brandt Professor of Engineering. In addition to his administrative work in the college, he was active in university-wide affairs and committees, including chairing the campus planning and space allocation committee. During his second year as dean he was stricken with cancer and after a short illness died on April 16, 2001.

Professor Robert Palumbo and his students designed a solar-powered chemical reactor which they tested at the Paul Scherrer Institut facility in Switzerland.

Among projects funded by the Three Goals – One Promise campaign were new furnishing in classrooms to replace the 40 year old tables and chairs that had served since the construction of Gellersen Center. Transparency projectors in classrooms were replaced with computer-based projectors and document cameras. Halls and classrooms were carpeted. Aided by a $200,000 National Science Foundation grant, a Scientific Visualization Lab was constructed. This facility allows users to view three dimensional objects from any angle using 3-D glasses and a system that locates the viewer's position. Air-conditioning of laboratories was completed. The electronics lab and the soil mechanics lab were completely remodeled and a computer-based engineering computation laboratory for civil and mechanical engineering was completed.

Two other recent initiatives are worth noting. Under the guidance of Professor Eric Johnson, who served for three years as the resident director of the Valparaiso international study center in Reutlingen, Germany, and the department of foreign languages, a full-year combination study and work experience in Reutlingen area industries has been developed for engineering students who also major or minor in German. A similar program was initiated in 2009 at EIGSI Engineering School in LaRochelle, France and one is under development at Zhejiang Institute of Technology in Hangzhou, China.

Kraig Joseph Olejniczak

Kraig Olejniczak began his engineering career as a freshman at Valparaiso University in 1983. A native of Green Bay, Wisconsin, he was born on February 6, 1965, and came to Valparaiso not only to study engineering but also to play football. He graduated with a degree in electrical engineering in 1987 and continued his engineering education at Purdue where he earned an M.S.E.E. in 1988 and a Ph.D. in 1991. From 1991 to 2002 he was a member of the electrical engineering faculty at the University of Arkansas, attaining the rank of professor in 2000. At

Five courses directly related to managing engineering work are taught by college of engineering faculty.

A second campaign – Our Valpo, Our Time – began its public phase in 2008. Included in this effort is a plan to modernize and relocate the manufacturing, materials testing, and heat power laboratories and to construct a significant laboratory addition on the south side of Gellersen to house modern computer-aided design laboratories. Construction is expected to begin in 2010.

Computers

In one way or another, both Dean Walesh and Dean Luecke spent considerable energy dealing with computers. By 1985 the impact of digital computing on engineering curricula had become a major concern. The difficult financial condition of the university in the 1970s had put Valparaiso somewhat behind leading engineering schools, a fact which ABET noted at its 1982 visit. With the Academic Computer Center (ACC) having responsibility for academic computing facilities, the college of engineering lacked direct control of computer laboratories used in its courses, thus requiring the faculty and deans to work both cooperatively and competitively with other units of the university to obtain needed computer hardware and software. Installation of 10 HP graphics computers by the ACC made it possible to begin the switch from pen-and-pencil engineering drawing to computer-aided drawing in 1986. Two years later, a complete PC classroom in the basement of Guild Hall

---

Arkansas he led the High Density Electronic Center's effort in power electronics miniaturization and packaging. In 1998 he received the Walter Fee Award from the IEEE Power Engineering Society as an outstanding young power engineer. At Arkansas he received awards for outstanding research and teaching.

Dr. Olejniczak began his service as dean of the college in 2002. He is the founder and chairman of Arkansas Power Electronics International, Inc., a firm commercializing high temperature micro electronic circuits for high power applications. He is co-author of *Elements of Wavelets for Engineers and Scientists* (Wiley, 2003).

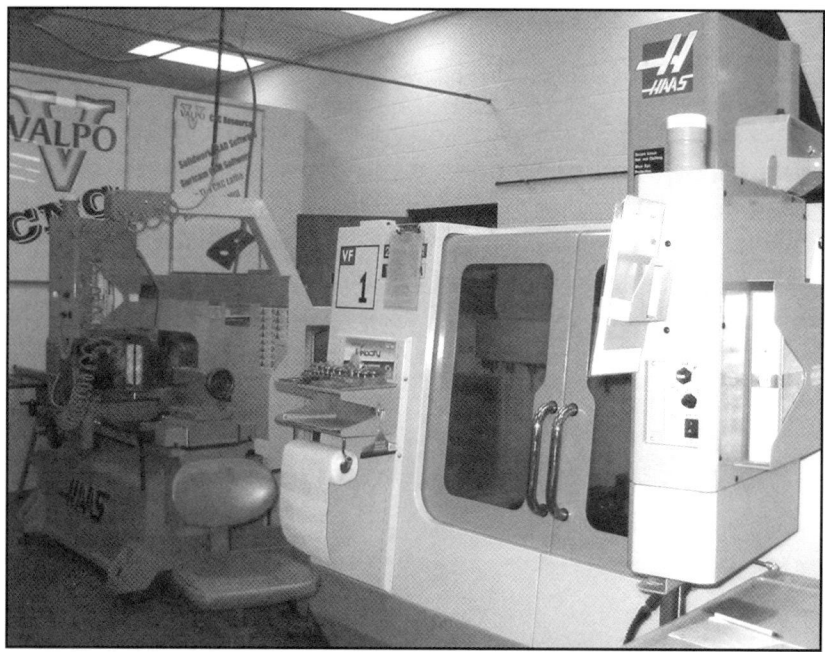

Numerically Controlled Tools in the Manufacturing Laboratory

was opened, and computer graphics took on a more significant role in the required drawing course. By 1989 all lab work in engineering drawing was done at this PC lab. The college made the first small move toward gaining control of its own computing facilities in 1991 when it converted a large classroom into the Gellersen Microcomputer and Work Station Laboratory. In the same year, the Data General MV8000 was replaced by a Digital Equipment VAX4000. Aided by a $75,000 grant from the Bethlehem Steel Foundation in 1996, the work station lab was updated to a UNIX-based Sun Microsystems server and SparcStation5 work stations. A second classroom was converted to a PC lab for use in mathematics and engineering courses. To smooth out the increasingly complex day-to-day operations of these computer facilities, the technical staff of the college assumed responsibility from the ACC for all operations in Gellersen except networks in 1996.

The rapid emergence of PC-based software in the mid-80s caused nearly continuous updating of course work and requirements. In 1985, the mechanical engineering department, under the leadership of Professor Lehmann, introduced PC-based data acquisition to its laboratories. In 1986, the ECE Department recommended that its students have their own PCs available for course work. To assist the ECE students and those in other majors that owned their own computers, a PC Resource Center, staffed by the college computer technician, was opened in 1987. By 1989 the ECE department's recommendation became a requirement. That same year the mathematics and computer science department introduced computer algebra, using the ACC laboratories, to the beginning calculus courses. Coincident with the engineering curriculum change in 1992, all new students were expected to have a PC at the end of their first semester. In 1994, the college began a program of bulk-purchase of PCs for resale to entering students at prices below retail. To aid freshmen with the still relatively high cost of PCs, the university offered an interest free loan to be repaid in four yearly installments. This program remained in effect until PCs had become a commodity for which bulk buying offered no cost advantage. By that time most entering students already owned a computer or had strong opinions about the specifications of the computer that they wanted.

One outcome of the shift to computers in the curriculum was the closing of the Engineering Supply Store, established by engineering students in the late 1940s to provide lower cost options for mechanical drawing equipment and quality slide rules. The demise of slide rules in the 1970s and the shift to computer-aided graphics in the early 1990s left the store with nothing to sell except low profit margin engineering paper and pencils. In earlier years the store netted yearly surpluses that helped fund student professional and social activities such as the annual banquet, but in its final years it did not make enough profit to pay the salary of the student manager. It was finally closed in 1995. With no drawing instruments needed, drafting tables also quickly became obsolete. In a short 40 years after Dean Hesse's Graland Hall was built to provide quality drafting room facilities, the last classroom containing drafting tables was converted to a regular classroom (much to the relief of students who found sitting on drafting stools at a drafting table for a lecture course a real challenge).

Professorships

Endowed professorships mark another way in which the College has steadily improved, as they contribute much of the salary and provide a yearly spending allowance to support the academic interests of the holder. The Richardsons' gift in 1984 established the Leitha and Willard Richardson Professorship. Willard Richardson was a long-time member of the board of directors, a civil engineering graduate of the University of Nebraska, and a principal in a construction firm in Omaha. The first holder of this professorship was Professor Demos Gelopulos; currently it is held by Professor P. Douglas Tougaw. Valparaiso electrical engineering graduate Fred Jenny served as a senior vice president of Unisys Corporation and as the president of one of its subsidiaries. To memorialize him after his untimely death, in 1993 his family created the Frederick F. Jenny Professorship of Emerging Technology. This professorship is awarded for a period of one or two years to pursue projects that will advance a professor's and the college's expertise in a new branch of technology. The first holder of this professorship was Professor Rodney Bohlmann. The Alfred W. Sieving Chair of Engineering was endowed in 1997 by Alfred Sieving's sisters to honor his

Electronics Laboratory-2009

career and love for Valparaiso. A 1935 Valparaiso mechanical engineering graduate, he spent his entire engineering career at the Caterpillar Corporation, where he was recognized as an outstanding mechanical designer. Professor John R. Steffen held this professorship from its inception until his retirement in 2008. Professor Robert D. Palumbo is the new Sieving Chair. Paul Brandt supported the university with many gifts. In the College of Engineering he is remembered by the Paul and Cleo Brandt Professorship of Engineering which was established in 1998 and was first awarded to Professor Gerald Seeley. The current holder is Associate Professor Eric Johnson.

A Changing of the "Old Guard"

As the College entered the new century, its faculty links to the early years of the reconstituted post-war college were almost gone. In the 1980s, becoming emeritus professors were William Shewan (1951-1983), Gerhard Vater (1956-1986), William Dauberman (1962-1987), Leslie Zoss (1958-1987), and Fred Kruger (1947-1989). A. Sami El-Naggar (1957-1990) retired early to devote full time to his environmental engineering consulting business. In the 1990s Gilbert Lehman (1956-1995), Merlyn Vocke (1955-1995), and James Schueler (1960-1997), all of whom had been Valparaiso students and faculty members in the 1950s, joined the ranks of emeriti professors. The retirement of Edgar Luecke (1955-2002) severed the last faculty link to the pre-Gellersen era of the College. Recently retired faculty members who had been students in the pre-Gellersen era are: Demos Gelopulos (1980-2003); John Steffen (1974-2008); and William Schoech (1970-2009).

TEN
A Look into the Future

Almost from the beginning, some kind of technical education has been a part of the offerings of Valparaiso University. During the earliest years it consisted of telegraphy and then surveying; later, courses in surveying and railroad engineering developed into a traditional civil engineering program. After a number of years, mechanical and electrical engineering were added, and when computers became an economic force, computer engineering was added. What does the future hold for the College of Engineering? New York Yankee catcher Yogi Berra is reputed to have said, "It's tough making predictions, especially about the future." One has only to follow the history of the video telephone and the Internet to be especially cautious. Almost all communications industry professionals in the 1960s were convinced that the video phone was the wave of the future, and Bell Laboratories allocated its best engineers to develop the infrastructure for such a service. It never found a market. Even today, when the video phone can be had almost at no cost with current Internet technology, it is used only rarely. These same communications professionals were involved in the early stages of Internet technology and almost none predicted its impact. So I present what follows with a great deal of caution, basing it on extrapolations of current trends. Probably the only sure prediction is that there will be a "game changing" development that no one predicted.

Ultimately, the future of the College of Engineering is linked to the future of Valparaiso University. If we can take anything from the first 150 years of its history, we can almost be sure that some event or situation will disrupt its current mission. How Valparaiso fares will depend on how it responds. The Methodist college, the Brown-Kinsey college, and the Lutheran college each developed a mission and constituency uniquely responsive to the needs of society for a time. The first two declined as they failed to respond adequately to society's changing needs and expectations. The present Lutheran version was founded to meet the higher education needs of a growing German immigrant church that was striving to move into mainstream American culture while maintaining the core of its separate identity. Four generations later, that goal is no longer relevant. Seeking to respond adequately once again, Valparaiso University has acknowledged its changed mission and is now actively considering ways in which its Lutheran understanding of Christianity and vocation can be the basis for an education attractive to new generations of parents and students. A continuing Lutheran emphasis on vocation will mean that professional and pre-professional programs should remain as a major component of the curriculum.

A potential disruption for both engineering and the university is the shift in the demographics of the American population. As the fraction of the population with Lutheran/European heritage declines, to grow and prosper, Valparaiso will spend a great deal of energy crafting its message and offerings to attract its share of an increasingly diverse student population. For the college of engineering, the challenge will be even greater. Historically, the ethnic groups in national ascendancy have shown less interest in engineering than their European predecessors. It remains to be seen if the present national sense of urgency to attract them will successfully reverse the decline of student interest in the sciences, technology, and engineering. The college has weathered enrollment challenges in the past; it may face even more difficult challenges in the future.

Possible visions for the future of engineering education can be seen in the new problems and concerns of society. As a problem solving profession, it is shaped by society's priorities for resource allocation, and the curriculum will reflect these national priorities. Historically, engineering work is divided into two entirely different activities. One is maintaining and improving mature technologies. The well-documented poor state of American infrastructure will require a steady supply of capital and creative engineers to achieve society's continued productivity, safety, and general well-being. The other work of engineers involves creating and developing new technologies that are not yet well defined or mature. Two of these emerging issues and opportunities that will influence the shape of engineering education are alternative energy sources to replace fossil fuels and the development of technologies in support of the life sciences and medicine. It is more difficult to predict the form of new technologies that will certainly arise due to the increasing power of computers. That which is not yet imagined may be reality in 20 years. The educational needs for these two types of engineering functions are somewhat in opposition, and crafting a curriculum to balance them will be achieved only through external pressure, spirited internal debate, and incremental changes.

In addition to these two different engineering functions, engineering curricula continue to change and evolve as technologies develop, mature, and even disappear. Of necessity, educators must deemphasize mature technologies and add courses in emerging technologies. In addition, the relative importance of various components of the curriculum also changes. Responses in the mid-20th century to national defense and space exploration priorities, financed by taxes, required a stronger science underpinning to the engineering curriculum and a corresponding deemphasis on economic design. The more recent emphasis on the engineer as an organizer and designer of economically viable products for the consumer and industrial market is now having its curricular impact. What is essential in the curriculum will always be open to debate.

What engineers do and how they do it is also changing. Essentially instantaneous computation and communication is revolutionizing the day-to-day work of engineers. Much of the difficult detailed analytical and experimental work necessary to craft a good engineering solution to a problem has been taken over by computer analysis and simulation. This increased productivity means that engineers will spend more time on concepts rather than details. In addition, rapid and worldwide communication has made it possible to move some engineering work to lower-cost engineers wherever they are in the world, and American engineers, especially, are being challenged to demonstrate the value that they add to products and services. To a greater extent, this added value will be in creating, directing, and managing intellectual property rather than in engineering details.

The necessary aptitudes and abilities of engineering students will continue to change as the proportion of American engineers needed for hands-on detailed work declines. The required mathematical and scientific sophistication continues to increase. As an example, an engineer's college mathematics studies once ended with calculus; they now begin with calculus. Subjects taught in graduate courses 30 years ago are now taught in an undergraduate's senior year. Many of the "how to" aspects of engineering have been shifted to engineering technologists who have been educated in four-year college-based engineering technology programs. At the same time, the liberal education that is necessary for management responsibilities remains essential. Engineering educators will continue to be challenged to craft a curriculum practical and specific enough to prepare graduates to be productive in their first job or graduate school and general enough to serve them as they become leaders twenty or thirty years hence.

The engineering profession continues to question whether the first engineering degree should produce a generalist or a specialist. Many now believe that the depth of knowledge needed to practice an engineering specialty can only be achieved by study at the graduate level and that the curriculum should prepare students for that career path. Yet there remain many valid engineering activities that require the skills and aptitudes of a generalist rather than a specialist. Many engineering graduates will continue to work toward advanced degrees in management or to pursue opportunities which do not lead to an engineering specialty. This internal tension will probably remain unresolved.

The history, character, and location of Valparaiso University all contribute to define for its College of Engineering a unique place in the spectrum of possible missions for engineering education. It will never be large enough to become a research institution or serve the needs of students with very narrow career interests. Not being located near the center of a major metropolitan center means that its mission will not be to serve the unique needs of a local economy. At the present time, the profession, working through ABET, seems to be willing to accept a variety of missions. The college will prosper by serving a constituency that values learning in a Christian community, desires a broader liberal rather than a narrower technical engineering education, and expects academic rigor. Valparaiso University is uniquely capable of delivering on these values, desires, and expectations.

Appendix A

Engineering Faculty – 1873-2009

This listing is limited to those who taught full time for at least one year.

Name	Years	Program
Bogarte, Martin	1873 - 1911	CE
Williams, Alpheus	1905 - 1927	CE
Lowrey, J. H.	1909 - 1911	CE
Yeoman, Ray	1909 - 1917	CE
Brownstein, Samuel	1910 - 1911	CE
Blackman, A. W.	1910 - 1911	CE
Turner, Frank	1910 - 1911	CE
Perkins, J. M.	1911 - 1912	CE
Muller, Henry	1911 - 1912	CE
Dougall, A. F.	1911 - 1912	CE
Hurme, Emil	1911 - 1913	CE
Klein, Elias	1911 - 1913	CE
Tucker, E. A.	1912 - 1913	CE
Weed, C. E.	1912 - 1913	CE
Forman, Louis	1913 - 1914	CE
Fischer, A. W.	1913 - 1914	CE
Crosland, Benjamin	1914 - 1915	CE
Tucker, Ernest	1914 - 1915	CE
Kellam, Fred	1914 - 1915	CE
Theroux, Frank	1914 - 1916; 1917 - 1923	CE
Snader, David	1914 - 1917	AE
Smalley, Arthur	1915 - 1916	CE
Burkhard, Paul	1915 - 1917	CE
Carlson, C. E.	1915 - 1917	CE
Dorr, Phillip	1916 - 1917	CE
Caulkins, H. J.	1917 - 1918	CE
Miller, Henry	1917 - 1918	CE
Reider, C. H.	1917 - 1920	CE
Fisher, Henry	1917 - 1920; 1922 - 1925	CE
Fager, Raymond	1918 - 1924	CE
Hanneman, H.	1919 - 1920	CE
Brown, Charles	1919 - 1921	CE
Carlton, Wilson	1920 - 1921	AE
McClure, Norman	1920 - 1921	CE

Uban, Moses	1920 - 1921; 1923 - 1960	ME
Winship, Ross	1920 - 1931	ME
Vaughn, Guy	1921 - 1922	CE
Trams, Theodore	1921 - 1923	CE
Bianchi, Joseph	1921 - 1924	CE
Durnall, William	1924 - 1925	CE
Greenwood, James	1924 - 1925	ME
Martin, F. R.	1925 - 1926	EE
Harvey, Howard	1925 - 1927	CE
Friedrich, Lawrence	1926 - 1928	CE
Lauritzen, Carl	1926 - 1940	EE
Bilger, Harry	1927 - 1930	CE
Blickensderfer, Herman	1927 - 1940	CE
Marzulli, Mario	1928 - 1929	EE
Peterson, Ernest	1929 - 1930	EE
Mallory, Donald	1929 - 1939; 1941 - 1943	EE
Taveira, Horace	1930 - 1933	ME
Moody, Howard	1930 - 1949	CE
Cushman, Paul	1933 - 1939	ME
Mummert, Harold	1943 - 1946	ME
Reuss, George	1946 - 1949; 1952 - 1955	EE
Kruger, Fred	1947 - 1989	ME
Kiser, Lewis	1948 - 1951	CE
Meyer, Robert	1948 - 1952	EE
Unnewehr, Lewis	1949 - 1955	EE
Hesse, Herman	1949 - 1972	ME
Peller, Charles	1949 - 1980	CE
Mortimer, Kenneth	1950 - 1987	CE
Frost, Daniel	1951 - 1952	CE
Shewan, William	1951 - 1983	EE
Chambers, Sherman	1952 - 1958	CE
Uban, Earl	1952 - 1959	CE
Keho, Clifford	1954 - 1956	CE
Fryberger, Elbert	1954 - 1957	ME
Vocke, Merlyn	1955 - 1995	EE
Luecke, Edgar	1955 - 2002	EE
Zippay, Michael	1956 - 1957	ME
Vater, Gerhard	1956 - 1986	EE
Lehmann, Gilbert	1956 - 1995	ME
Yunghans, Charles	1957 - 1961	EE
Bolden, D. Ira	1957 - 1962	CE
Weston, Ernest	1957 - 1962	EE
Isbell, Robert	1957 - 1974	ME
Marino, Robert	1958 - 1961; 1965 - 1974	CE
Zoss, Leslie	1958 - 1986	ME

List, Kurt	1960 - 1969	ME
ElNaggar, A. Sami	1960 - 1990	CE
Schueler, James	1960 - 1997	CE
Sorensen, Robert	1962 - 1963	CE
Koller, David	1962 - 1966	EE
Dauberman, William	1962 - 1987	EE
Richard, O. Donnie	1963 - 1965	CE
Krabec, Glen	1963 - 1966	EE
Marin, John	1964 - 1965	CE
Hartwigsen, Christian	1964 - 1965	ME
Hahn, William	1964 - 1966; 2005 - 2006	ME
Jud, Henry	1964 - 1968	EE
Kempf, Dale	1964 - 1969; 1990- 2009	EE
Huang, Wen-Hsiung	1965 - 1966	CE
Keplar, Richard	1965 - 1969	CE
Lux, George	1966 - 1976	ME
Swanson, Robert	1968 - 1969	EE
Walesh, Stuart	1968 - 1970; 1985 - 1999	CE
Halter, Matthew	1969 - 1970	EE
Turley, Charles	1969 - 1970	ME
Weiss, Marvin	1969 - 1973	ME
Rose, Robert	1969 - 1991	ME
Schoech, William	1970 - 2009	ME
Khanna, Jagennath	1970 - 1971	CE
Hart, Dan	1970 - 1972; 1979 -	EE
Sureshwara, Bangalore	1971 - 1972	CE
Spring, Brad	1971 - 2001	CE
Steffen, John	1974 - 2008	ME
Herron, William	1974 - 1976	ME
Bohlmann, Rodney	1975 - 1994	EE
Doria, Michael	1977 - 2009	ME
Kusch, Lloyd	1977 - 1978	ME
Heuer, Charles	1977 - 1980	ME
Crosmer, Joel	1977 - 1980 ; 1984 - 1990	EE
Turner, Richard	1978 - 1979	EE
Frankus, Andrew	1978 - 1980	ME
Lauck, Francis	1978 - 1980	ME
Savur, Vivek	1978 - 1981	CE
Streit, Donald	1980 - 1982	ME
Scroggin, James	1980 - 1985	ME
Longinow, Anatol	1981 - 1982	CE
Torczynski, Cynthia	1981 - 1982	EE
Szarkowicz, Donald	1981 - 1983	EE
Radwan, Abdul-Khalek	1981 - 1983	ME
Salim, Abdul	1981 - 1984	CE

Jensen, Norman	1981 - 1998	ME
Gelopulos, Demos	1981 - 2003	EE
Kakar, A. Tosh	1982 - 1985	EE
Ahmadi, Nasser	1982 - 1989	ME
Seeley, Gerald	1983 - 2001	CE
Bunnett, Cheryl	1984 - 1985	EE
Igga-Musisi, Patrick	1984 - 1986	EE
Kraft, L. Alan	1985 -	EE
Saboury, Saeed	1985 - 1987	ME
Thompson, Harold	1985 - 1990	CE
Goodman, Daniel	1985 - 2006	EE
Franck, Robert	1986 - 1987	EE
Palumbo, Robert	1987 -	ME
Grundmeier, Daniel	1987 - 1988	EE
Johnson, Eric	1987 - 1988; 1996 -	EE
Moldenhauer, Paul	1988 - 1989	ME
Bora, Bipin	1990 - 1995	ME
Tarhini, Kasim	1990 - 2001	CE
AlJobeh, Zuhdi	1991 -	CE
Surma, David	1991 - 1993; 1995 - 1996	EE
Yap, SinMin	1995 - 1997	ME
Tougaw, P. Douglas	1996 -	EE
Weiss, Peter	1996 -	CE
Lehmann, Susan	1997 - 1998	CE
Guo, Raymond	1997 - 1998	ME
Malicky, David	1998 - 2002	ME
Schmucker, Douglas	1998 - 2003	CE
Barrett, Michael	1998 - 2003	ME
Bhonsle, Suryaji	1999 - 2003	ME
Polito, Carmine	2001 -	CE
Will, Jeffrey	2001 -	EE
Olejniczak, Kraig	2002 -	EE
Stone, Wesley	2002 - 2004	ME
Leitch, Kenneth	2003 - 2008	CE
Hagenberger, Michael	2004 -	CE
Johnson, Peter	2004 -	ME
Freeman, Richard	2004 - 2008	EE
Sevener, Kathleen	2005 -	ME
Budnik, Mark	2006 -	EE
Duncan, G. Scott	2006 -	ME
Zimmerman, Karl	2007 -	CE
Hwang, Yeonsang	2007 -	CE

Appendix B

Department Heads and Chairs

Starting in 1957, the College of Engineering was administratively organized into three departments. The title "Head" was later changed to "Chair."

Civil Engineering

Peller, Charles	1957 – 1979
Spring, Bradford	1979 – 1986; 1991 – 1998
Seeley, Gerald	1987 – 1991; 1998 – 1999
Tarhini, Kassim	1999 – 2001
AlJobeh, Zuhdi	2001 – 2003
Weiss, Peter	2003 – 2007
Hagenberger, Michael	2007 –

Electrical and Computer Engineering

Shewan, William	1957 – 1973
Luecke, Edgar	1973 – 1985; 1988 – 1991
Gelopulos, Demosthenes	1986 – 1988; 1991 – 2001
Tougaw, P. Douglas	2001 –

Mechanical Engineering

Kruger, Fred	1957 – 1965
Zoss, Leslie	1966 – 1976
Schoech, William	1976 – 1981
Steffen, John	1981 – 1991; 1997 – 2005
Palumbo, Robert	1991 – 1993; 1994 – 1997; 2005 – 2008
Doria, Michael	1993 – 1994
Johnson, Peter	2008 –

Appendix C

Engineering National Council Members 2002-2008

Name	Class	
Linda L. Allen	1978	ME
Jill K. Bensen	1983	CE
James R. Beyreis	1966	CE
Cary T. Conrad	1979	EE
John L. Draheim	1964	EE
Stephen A. Furbacher	1970	ME
Eugene P. Holland	1957	CE
F. Peter Jenny	1985	EE
Ralph W. Johnson	1959	CE
Kenneth H. Kastman	1966	EE
Paul L. Kruelle	1963	EE
Richard L. Landry	1986	EE
David A. Lange	1981	CE
Philip B. Leege	1957	ME
Charles F. Lieske	1970	ME
Andrew N. Nunnemaker	1991	EE
Timothy W. Paul	1976	EE
Duane C. Rabe	1976	EE
Jeffrey A. Raday	1979	CE
Gary L. Rosenbeck	1971	CE
Robert J. Schickel	1971	CE
Ronald G. Schultz	1953	EE
T. Carl Schwan	1966	ME
Craig W. Selover	1971	ME
Roger D. Sims	1965	CE
Edward W. Tornberg	1955	EE
Kristen E. Yakimow	1991	EE
John W. Yakimow	1964	ME
Kim A. Zeile	1977	ME
Larry W. Zimmerman	1970	CE

Appendix D

Alumni Association Board Members

Name	Class	
Charles A. Bischoff	1968	EE
Kevin L. Boettcher	1979	ME
Norman L. Conrad	1962	CE
Jonathan A. DeMik	1997	ME
Ernest E. Heuer, Jr.	1959	CE
Arnold A. Hilgenkamp	1959	ME
Michael C. Jensen	1994	EE
Carmen Kimber Jones	1990	EE
Paul M. Jud	1986	EE
Eugene H. Kanning	1961	CE
John Krause	1961	EE
Thomas L. Luekens	1964	EE
Kip A. Macke	1980	CE
Thomas E. Madden	1982	EE
Robert J. Miller	1959	EE
Robert C. Moellering	1933	CE
Andrew N. Nunemaker	1991	EE
John M. Oelschlaeger	1980	EE
Alan R. Pretzel	1960	ME
Kenneth C. Rakow, Sr.	1967	ME
Marvin F. Rammelsberg	1952	ME
William C. Rohn	1940	ME
William F. Rolf	1958	ME
Charles T. Rolf	1954	ME
Lambert J. Runge	1958	EE
Paul Rupprecht, Jr.	1956	ME
Joseph P. Sauer	1971	EE
John P. Schoening	1974	ME
Robert C. Storbeck	1951	ME
Clarence R. Strutz	1933	ME
William R. Tatman	1940	CE
Frederick W. Thiele	1957	CE
Michael J. VanBeek	1982	ME
Hubert H. Velepec	1955	ME
Andrea Hoth Warp	2000	ME
Ronald H. Zech	1965	EE

Appendix E

Degree and Enrollment Data

Degree and enrollment data has been compiled from two sources. For the period before 1951, degree data was obtained from commencement programs and catalog lists. During the 1910s, both Bachelor and Engineer degrees were awarded. The data presented represents the sum of these two. There is some overlap in these two numbers as some students took the Bachelor degree and then stayed for another year and earned the Engineer degree. After 1916 only the Engineer degree was awarded until 1924 when the degree name was changed to Bachelor. For the post 1951 era, numbers were obtained from lists of graduates maintained by the college of engineering.

The data is presented as lines connecting data points rather than tables so that trends, if any, can be more easily spotted. What is most striking about the data is the high variability that is superimposed on longer term trends. The post-1951 numbers for each year are for calendar years rather than academic years. Until 1971, mid-term graduation was in January instead of December. The introduction of cooperative education in 1983 resulted in delayed graduation for those that selected the coop sequence. These two discontinuities in the data are small compared to the general variability. Over the full number of years that each degree was offered, the average for each degree is: CE, 18.5; EE, 23.6; ME, 26.2; and CpE, 4.6.

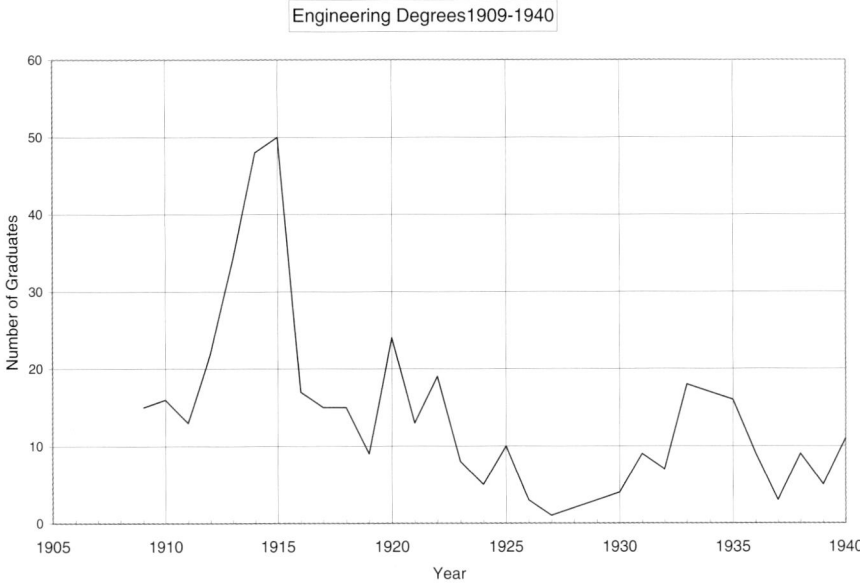

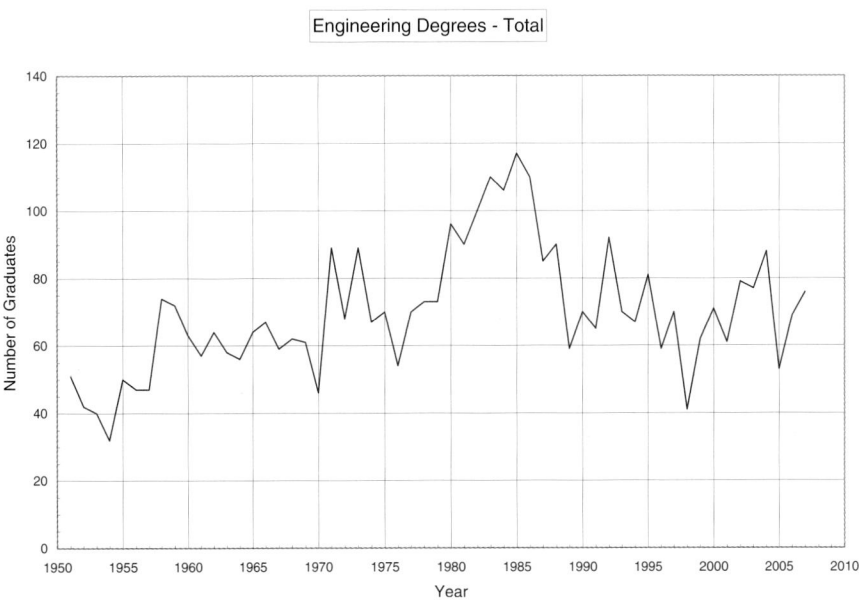

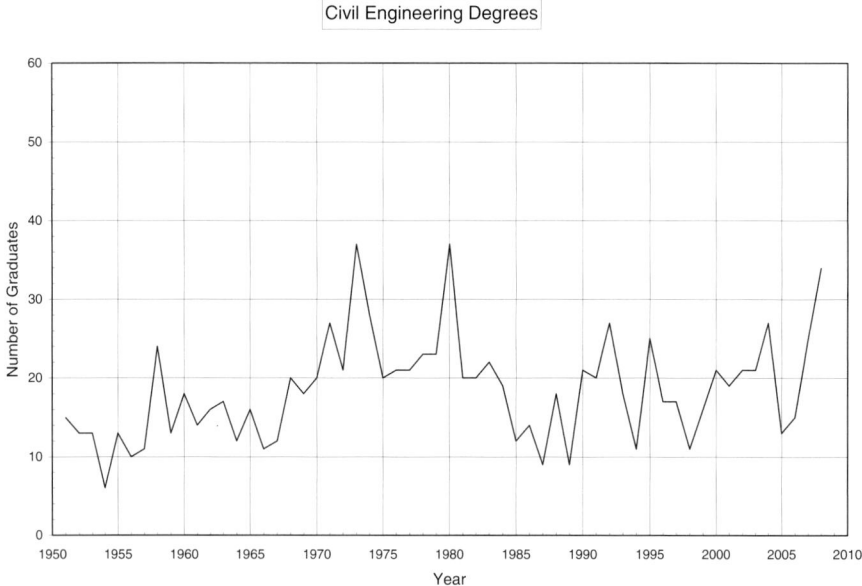

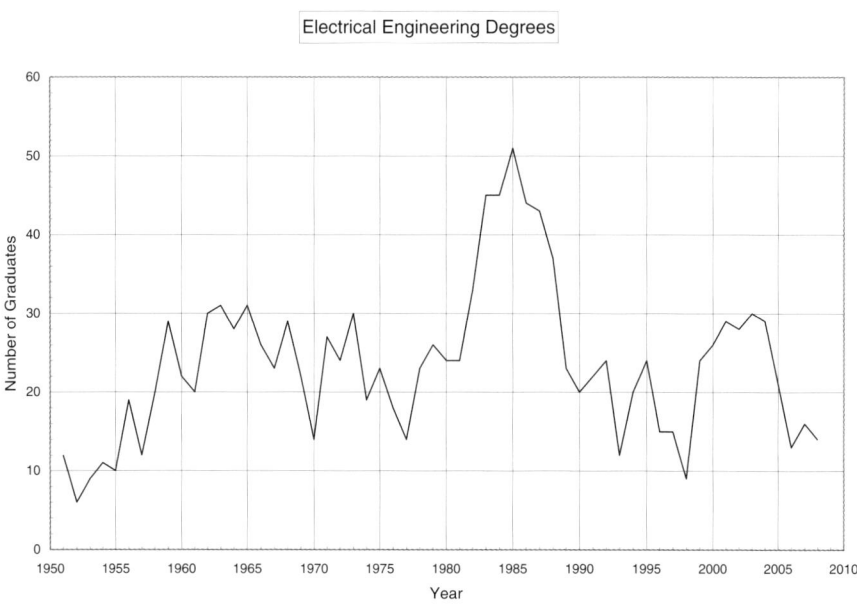

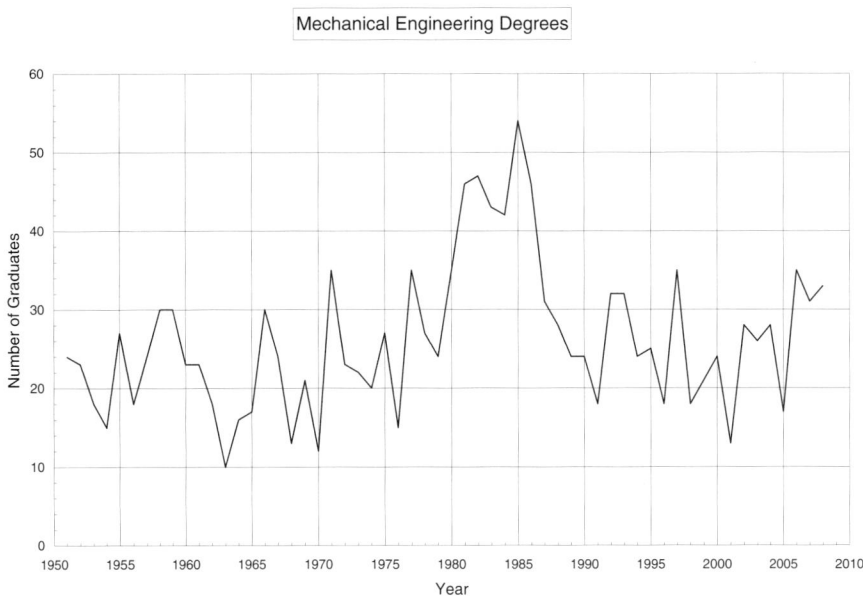

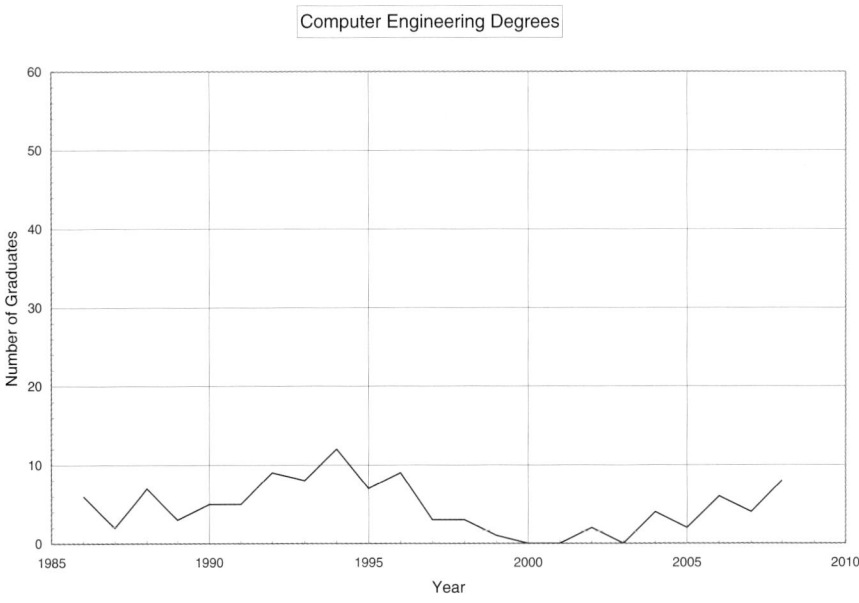

REFERENCES

Extensive use was made of catalogs, newspapers, year books, official minutes, and personal files in the archive of Valparaiso University. Major sources are referenced in the text. Except for those provided by the individuals themselves, photographs are from the university archive or the author.

Albers, James W. *From Centennial to Golden Anniversary — The History of Valparaiso University from 1959 – 1975.* Valparaiso, IN: Valparaiso University, 1976.

Baepler, Richard. *Flame of Faith, Lamp of Learning.* St. Louis, MO: Concordia Publishing House, 2001.

Boone, Richard G. *History of Education in Indiana*, Indianapolis, IN: Reprint of 1872 edition by Indiana Historical Bureau, 1941.

Goodspeed, Weston and Blanchard, Charles (Editors). *Counties of Porter and Lake, Indiana, Historical and Biographical.* Chicago: F. A. Battey & Co., 1882.

Grayson, Lawrence P. "A Brief History of Engineering Education in the United States." *Engineering Education*, (December, 1977).

Grayson, Lawrence P. *The Making of an Engineer — An Illustrated History of Engineering Education in the United States and Canada.* New York: John Wiley, 1993.

Grinter, Linton E. "Report of the Committee on Evaluation of Engineering Education (1952-1955)." *Journal of Engineering Education*, Vol. 46, no. 1, (September, 1955).

Hammond, Harold P. (Editor). "Report of Committee on Aims and Scope of Engineering Curricula." *Journal of Engineering Education Vol. 30 No. 7,* (March 1940).

History of Porter County, Volume II. Chicago and New York: Lewis Publishing Co., 1912.

Mann, Charles R. *A Study of Engineering Education, Prepared for the Joint Committee on Engineering Education of the National Engineering Societies. Bulletin Number Eleven,* New York: Carnegie Foundation, 1918.

Meiksins, Peter. "Professionalism and Conflict: The Case of the American Association of Engineers." *Journal of Social History* (2001).

Prados, John W. (Editor). A *Proud Legacy of Quality Assurance in the Preparation of Technical Professionals — ABET 75th Anniversary Retrospective.* Baltimore MD: ABET Inc., 2007.

Smith, William B. (Editor). *Education Year-Book 1872.* New York: A. S. Barnes & Co, 1872.

Stratton, Julius A. and Mannix, Loretta H. *Mind and Hand – The Birth of MIT.* Cambridge, MA: MIT Press, 2005.

Stimpson, George W. "The Story of Valparaiso University – Including an Account of the Recent Period of Turbulence." Published by the author, 1921.

Strietelmeier, John. *Valparaiso's First Century.* Valparaiso, IN: Valparaiso University, 1959.

Thomas, Roland E. "Accreditation Perspectives – A Historical Note (1998 Reprint)." *The Interface – A publication of IEEE* (April, 2006).

Wickenden, William E. (Editor). *Report of the Investigation of Engineering Education, 1923 – 1929, Vol. 1.* Society for the Promotion of Engineering Education, 1930.

INDEX

ABET, 148-149, 151-152
academic computer center, 113, 136, 167
aims and scope of engineering curricula, 76-77
Allen, Linda Ivett, 146
Alten's foundry, 83
Alumni Hall, 119
American Association of Engineers, 37, 57
American College of Dental Surgery, 26
American College of Medicine, 25, 40
American Institute of Electrical Engineers, 22
American Society of Civil Engineers, 114
American Society for Engineering Education, 23, 41, 107
American Society of Mechanical Engineers, 22, 114
Appian Society, 114
architectural engineering, 33, 47, 113
Arts-Law Building, 38, 106
Art-Music Building, 122
Art-Psychology Building, 123
Atomic Energy Commission, 106
Auditorium Building, 17, 111
Azman, Bill, 94
Aepler, Richard, 122

Baldwin, Mantie, 12
Baldwin Hall, 36, 132
Baier, Peter, 91
Bauer, John C., 52
Beggs, James, 122
Benton Hall, 132
Bethlehem Steel Foundation, 168
Besozzi, Leo, 162
Beumer, Richard, 118, 162
Beyreis, James, 118
Bilger, Harry E., 55-56
Black, Homer, 28
Blickensderfer, Herman, 77
board of instruction, 11
Bogarte Book Store, 17, 36
Bogarte, Martin E., 11, 12, 15-18, 19, 25, 27, 34, 37
Bohlmann, Rodney, 141, 155, 170
Brandt Hall, 119
Brandt, Paul, 72, 102
Brandt pofessorship, 171
Branco, 102

Bretscher, Manuel, 106
Brown, Charles C., 46
Brown, Henry B., 10, 11, 25, 26, 38, 39, 44
Brown, Henry K., 39-40, 44-45
Brown, Kinsey B., 117

Caterpillar Foundation, 162
Centennial Exhibition, 20
Center for the Arts, 161
Center for Entrepreneurship, 164
Chapel Hall, 17
Chapel of the Resurrection, 111
chemical engineering, 33
Christopher Center, 162
Cincinnati, Univ. of, 42
Civil Engineering Dept., 12, 19, 29
Civil Engineering Society, 37
Claussen, Howard, 118
Cloud, John, 28
Cold War, 101,124
College of Applied Science, 46
College of Engineering, 63-64, 81, 92
Colley, Glen, 89, 91
Commerce Hall, 7, 35, 55, 132
commercial engineering, 56
computer-aided drawing, 167
computer engineering, 143-144, 155-156
computer science, 144
co-operative education, 143
co-operative plans, 70
Crusade for Valparaiso U., 152
curriculum
  VMFC, 4
  1880, 13
  CE degree, 30-33
  Arch. Engr., 33
  1927, 54
  1949, 97-98
  1958-64, 114-116
  1970s, 137-142
  1990s, 157-159
Cushman, Paul, 64, 71

Data General MV8000, 168
Dau, William H. T., 52
Dau and Kreinheder Halls, 103, 119
Dauberman, William, 171
Deaconess Hall, 119
DEC VAX4000, 168

Delaware, Univ. of, 87
DeMotte Hall, 38
Dodge, G. A., 4, 11, 16, 19
Dodge Institute of Telegraphy, 19
Domestic Science Building, 38, 40
Doria, Michael, 136
dorms A, B, and C, 103
Dorrough, Lorraine Gaunt, 146
Draheim, John, 118
East Hall, 16
EC2000, 149, 152, 163
ECPD accreditation, 110, 111, 147-148
Engineers Council for Professional Development, 58-61, 69, 74-76, 102
Ecole Centrale, 8
Ecole Polytechnique, 5, 14
Eggers, T. C., 96
ElNaggar, A. Sami, 113, 171
Engineering Annex Building, 84, 123
Engineering Annual, 37
Engineering Building, 55, 83-84, 93, 103, 132
Engineering Department, 11, 15, 19, 22, 36, 53, 63
Engineering Laboratory Building, 88-89, 92-93, 102, 107, 123
Engineering Foundation, 109
Engineering Society, 99
Engineering Supply Store, 99, 169
engineering technology, 124
engineering train, 99
Evans, Horace, 50
Evansville Plan, 69

Federal Housing Authority, 111
Fisher, Henry T., 51, 53
Fites, Donald, 118, 162
Fleck, Paul, 111
Flint Hall, 16
Forward to the Eighties, 133
Foundry Annex, 36, 106
Freeman, Azariah, 3
Friedrich, Walter G. 68, 74
Furbacher, Stephen, 118
Future Engineers Week, 135

Gellersen Center, 120-122, 162
Gellersen, William, 120, 122-125
Gellersen work station lab, 168
Gelopulos, Demos, 118, 146, 155, 170, 171
GI Bill, 80, 84, 102

Goals of Engineering Education, 117, 125-126, 135
Goodman, Daniel, 146
Graebner, Norman, 129
Graland Hall, 55, 107, 123
Gray, Wilbur, 99
Grinter report, 107, 109-110, 125
Guild and Memorial Halls, 80, 84, 91

Harre, Alan, 153
Harre Union, 111
Hart, Daniel, 136
Harvey, Howard D., 53
Hawkins, Blair, 89, 91
Heine Hall, 94
Heine, Leonard, 91. 94
Heimlich Hall, 36
Henrichs, Karl, 120
Heritage Hall, 17
Hesse, Helen, 162
Hesse, Herman, 92, 93, 95, 96, 102, 104-106, 112-113, 121
Hesse Learning Resource Center, 162, 164
Higher Education Facilities Act, 120, 121
Hild, Carol, 117
Hilltop Gymnasium, 74, 120
Hodgdon, Daniel R., 40, 44
Holland, Eugene, 118
HP 3000II, 137
Huegli, Albert G., 129-130, 136
Huegli Hall, 119, 153

IBM 1620, 136
IBM 1710, 136
Illinois Industrial University, 14
industrial engineering, 113
industrial research and development, 112
International Carpenters Union, 90
Institute of Electrical and Electronics Engineers, 114
Institute of Radio Engineers, 114
International students, 31, 160-161
Isbell, Robert, 113
Instrument for Internal Governance, 130

Jenny, Frederick, 118
Jenny Professorship, 118, 170
Jensen, Norman, 143
Johnson, Eric, 166, 171
Johnson, Ralph, 118, 162
Jud, Henry, 118

Kallay-Christopher Hall, 162
Kempf, Dale, 118
Kinsey Hall fire, 131
Kinsey, Oliver P. 39, 40
Kiser, Lewis, 87
Klingsick Addition, 132
Klopp, Ruth, 117
Kraft, L. Alan, 146
Kreinheder, Oscar C., 52, 63, 65, 67
Kretzmann Hall, 120, 153
Kretzmann, Otto P., 79, 82, 85, 86, 90, 96, 105, 120
Kroencke, Frederick W., 65, 67, 68
Kroencke Hall, 94-95, 101
Kruger, Fred W., 81, 91, 105, 112, 113, 118-119, 120, 121, 134, 136, 171
Ku Klux Klan, 50

Lankenau Hall, 119
land grant universities, 8
Larson, Raymond, 84
Lauritzen, Carl W., 71
law department, 16
LeBien Hall, 132
Lehmann, Gilbert M., 113, 118, 134-136, 169, 171
Lighting the Way, 161
Lilly Endowment, 111
Longinow, Anatol, 118
Lowry, H., 34
Luecke, Edgar J., 113, 118, 136, 156-157, 159
Lutheran Church-Missouri Synod, 132
Lutheran Deaconess Association, 119, 152
Lutheran Layman's League, 95-96
Lutheran University Association, 162

Mallory, Donald D., 55, 71, 81-82
Mann Report, 14, 41, 56, 64
Manning, Armin, 106
manual training department, 35
Martin, F. R., 53
Master of Engineering Management, 166
Masters programs, 113, 117, 135
McCall, Ethel and Merle, 32
Medical Building, 26, 36, 55, 94
Medsger, Alton T., 55
Meier Hall, 121
Meitz, Alger, 118
Meyer, Robert, 97
Michalk, Erwin, 91

MIT, 7, 12, 14, 22, 68
Moeller, Marilyn, 117
Moellering Library, 111, 162
Moellering, Margaret, 111
Moellering, Robert, 72, 95
Moody, Howard W., 63-65, 71, 81, 97
Moody Laboratory, 85, 123
Morgan, Gale, 91
Morgan, Milan, 88, 91
Morrill Act, 5, 8
Mortimer, Kenneth, 113
Muhlenbruch, Carl, A. 85, 86
Mummert, Harold, 97

National Defense Education Act, 110
National Science Foundation, 109, 113, 165
National Society of Professional Engineers, 58
Neils Science Center, 120-122
North Central Association, 52, 72
Northern Indiana Normal School, 10-11, 16
Norwich University, 6
Ohio Northern University, 103
Old College Building, 35, 50, 52
Olejiniczak, Kraig, 165
orientation courses, 138-139
Our Valpo, Our Time, 167

Palumbo, Robert, 166
PC Resource Center, 169
Peller, Charles G., 97, 107, 112, 113, 134, 136, 143
Pelzer, Gerald, 118
Pharmacy, College of, 67-68
physics department, 116
Prentice, D. B., 87
Purdue University, 9, 68
Purdue-Valparaiso co-op program, 82

Rensselaer Polytechnic Institute, 6, 14
Reuss, George, 78-88 91, 97
Richardson Professorship, 170
Rose Hulman, 9
Rose Polytechnic Institute, 27, 87
Rose, Robert, 136
Rubke, Walter, 130

Sandborg, Kathryn, 117
School of Engineering, 33, 46, 48
School of Co-Industrial Engineering, 46

Science Building, 25, 74, 98
scientific course, 4, 11, 15, 19, 29
scientific visualization lab, 166
Sheele Hall, 119
Schanbel Hall, 145
Schnabel, Robert, 136, 152
Schoech, William, 118, 136, 171
Schueler, James, 113, 114, 118, 171
Schultz, Barbara, 117
Schwann, T. C. Jr., 118
Scribner, Albert, 65, 80, 86, 91
Scroggin, James, 143, 144-145, 153
Seeley, Gerald, 146, 163-165, 171
Shewan, William, 112, 113, 134, 136, 139-139, 143, 171
Sieving, Alfred, 72
Sieving Chair, 170
Sims, Roger, 118
slide rules, 137
Snader, David, 32
Society for the Promotion of Engineering Education
see American Society for Engineering Education
Society of Women Engineers, 146
Sorenson, John, 137
Spring, Bradford, 136
Sputnik, 107, 109
Steffen, John, 118, 136, 171
Stevens Institute of Technology, 22
Sun Microsystems, 168
SWTP computer, 141

Tanck, Paul, 107
Tatman, William, 72
Tau Beta Pi, 114, 117
tax-supported public education, 2, 10
TED, 99
telegraphy, 4
Terre Haute School of Industrial Science, 9, 31

Theroux, Frank, 32, 48, 49
Thomas, Ancil, 82, 106
Three Goals – One Promise, 161, 163, 166
Thrun, Walter, 82
Tornberg, Edward, 118, 162
Tougaw, P. Douglas, 170

Uban, Moses W., 52, 71,81, 82, 84, 86, 91, 96-98
United States Military Academy, 5
Unnewehr, Lewis, 97
Urschel Hall, 133

Valparaiso College, 25
Valparaiso Male and Female College, 1, 10
Valparaiso Technical Institute, 19
Valparaiso Union, 120
Vater, Gerhard, 113, 171
Venture of Faith film, 96
vocational training program, 51
Vocke, Merlyn C., 113, 118, 171
Virginia, Univ. of, 7

Walesh, Stuart, 114, 118, 153-155, 159
Wehrenberg Hall, 119
Wesemann Hall, 120, 132
Wickenden report, 58-61, 64, 74
Wickenden, W. E., 58, 71
Williams, Alpheus A., 28, 34, 37
Winship, Ross, 53
Woike, Otto, 94
Worcester Free Institute, 21
Worcester Polytechnic, 27

Yeoman, Ray C., 30-31, 37
Yakimow, John, 118

Zoss, Leslie, 112, 113, 130, 134, 136, 143, 171
Zech, Ronald, 118